THE ANCIENT MARINER SPEAKS

THE ANCIENT MARINER SPEAKS

Examining Regimes of Truth in ADHD

MARION STORDY

Fernwood Publishing • Halifax & Winnipeg

Editing: Brenda Conroy
Cover design: John van der Woude
Printed and bound in Canada by Hignell Book Printing

Published in Canada by Fernwood Publishing
32 Oceanvista Lane
Black Point, Nova Scotia, B0J 1B0
and 748 Broadway Avenue, Winnipeg, Manitoba, R3G 0X3
www.fernwoodpublishing.ca

Fernwood Publishing Company Limited gratefully acknowledges the financial support
of the Government of Canada through the Canada Book Fund and the Canada Council for the Arts,
the Nova Scotia Department of Communities, Culture and Heritage,
the Manitoba Department of Culture, Heritage and Tourism under the
Manitoba Publishers Marketing Assistance Program and the Province of Manitoba,
through the Book Publishing Tax Credit, for our publishing program.

Library and Archives Canada Cataloguing in Publication

Stordy, Marion
The ancient mariner speaks : examining regimes
of truth in ADHD / Marion Stordy.

(Fernwood basics)
Includes bibliographical references.
ISBN 978-1-55266-471-1

1. Attention-deficit hyperactivity disorder.
2. Attention-deficit-disordered children.
I. Title. II. Series: Fernwood basics

RJ506.H9S76 2012   618.92'8589   C2011-908396-5

CONTENTS

ACKNOWLEDGMENTS

My thanks first to Gerald, my husband of many years, who has been my rock throughout what must have seemed to him a never-ending process. I could never have undertaken this work without his support.

Thanks also to my children and their partners: Larry and Wendy, Allan and Noella, Cheryl and Darrell, Paul and Cathy, Mary Margaret and Jody. They have been lavish in their praise for my efforts, yet have managed to keep me grounded and humble, as one's children tend to do.

Thank-you to my twelve grandchildren, who provided me with a glimpse into and greater understanding of the fast changing world of children.

I must acknowledge Dr. Gail Jardine, whose work helped to make Foucault more accessible to me.

I owe a great debt of gratitude to my friend and mentor, Dr. Fiona Walton. Without her timely advice, encouragement and support, I can truthfully say I would never have completed this book.

For my grandson Benjamin, who inspired me to write this book.

THE ANCIENT MARINER SPEAKS

That moment that his face I see
I know the man that must hear me:
To him my tale I teach.
(Coleridge 1798, *The Rime of the Ancient Mariner*)

I call myself the "Ancient Mariner" half in fun and wholly in earnest. For readers not familiar with eighteenth-century romantic poetry, the Ancient Mariner, the leading character in a poem by S.T. Coleridge, was an old sailor who felt the need to tell his tragic story over and over to anyone he could persuade to stop and listen to him. Like the protagonist in Coleridge's composition, I too feel compelled to tell my story. The albatross around my neck may not be as visible to the naked eye as the bird the Ancient Mariner was forced to carry, yet it is just as real. My albatross is the misery endured by the many children labelled attention deficit hyperactivity disorder (ADHD) in the school system and, more specifically, the misery endured by my grandson during his journey through that education system, having been labelled ADHD soon after he entered the grade one classroom. And this albatross will remain around my neck until I tell my story to those who have the ability to remove it. Therefore, the "telling of my tale" has a purpose, as I trust that it will contribute to the demise of this particular albatross, so that it will no longer haunt classrooms, crushing the spirit of countless innocent children. The "wedding guests" I am urging to listen to me are not a group of people gathered to witness a nuptial celebration, as in Coleridge's poem, but consist of all those involved in the education of children. My hope is that my story will touch the hearts and minds of those with power over children's education, in such a way that they will gain a little more under-standing of how certain decisions that have been made, particularly in the areas of testing and labelling, have had such a negative impact on some children. I trust too that parents and caregivers of children who have suffered from this practice of labelling will read it and gain some comfort from knowing that they are not alone. My tale, which I tell narratively and autoethnographically, is a combination of the experiences of three generations: my own, my son's and my grandson's. It describes the way that changes in discourse and understanding affect the school experiences of children in my own family.

The process of thinking about and writing this story has forced me to reflect deeply about myself and all the beliefs and practices which were part of the culture of the era in which I was born and raised and, in turn, raised my children. I have discovered much about myself, reinforcing for me the reflexive value of narrative. Until I engaged in this writing process, I never considered myself a person who questioned society's dictates but rather a well-behaved, obedient young woman of my time, one who blindly obeyed, with a mindset similar to that of the ill-fated troops in Tennyson's famous *Charge of the Light Brigade* (1854: 1035), "Theirs not to reason why, Theirs but to do or die." However, reflecting on my life has made me realize that I am probably more assertive than I envision; otherwise I would not have chosen such a controversial topic for my book. I suspect that motherhood brought out the latent assertiveness in me, since I was determined that my children would enjoy more choices and benefits than I had. Sometimes this caused conflict with my husband, and even though it was in my nature to avoid conflict, I did not back down if it was an issue which affected my children. The well being of children, particularly my own children and grandchildren, has always been a major concern for me. I daresay my feelings are shared by most mothers and grandmothers. We celebrate or we suffer, we rejoice or we agonize, according to the fortunes of our progeny. But perhaps I should hesitate to make such an assumption. The fact that not everybody feels the way I do was one of the frustrations with which I struggled throughout my life. I often failed to conform to society's dictates about how I was supposed to feel — as a child, as a young woman, as a wife, as a mother. One example was my first experience of motherhood, compared to the myth that mothers experience an instant rush of love and tenderness from the first moment they gaze on their infant. I had been told that is the way I would feel, and that is what I expected. To my surprise and bafflement, I felt nothing but relief that the ordeal was over, and it took a while for me to find that unconditional motherly love. Now I realize that it was a perfectly normal reaction, exacerbated no doubt by the fact that I'd had a very difficult delivery, thousands of miles from my home, surrounded by strangers, in what one could almost call hostile territory. Also I am a person who needs some time to react to new experiences. And through the years I have met other mothers who felt the way I did at their first birthing. Yet at the time I wondered despairingly what was wrong with me. I was subscribing to what the French philosopher Michel Foucault (1926–1984) called a "regime of truth" of that epoch. It was assumed that everybody was cut from the same cloth and that, if a person deviated from the expected pattern, obviously there was something wrong with the person, not the pattern. I think now that I secretly resented that suggestion all my life, even as I struggled to conform because I didn't want to be outside the pale. That, I suppose, is one of the reasons I feel so strongly about children being made to feel out of place in the classroom, which should foster a sense of belonging, since it is "the only societal institution designed exclusively for children" (Cohen 2006: 13). That too is doubtless why I was initially attracted to the writings of Foucault, since he advocates that we become responsibly aware of how we enact or resist the norms fabricated by society.

Bringing Michel Foucault into the Picture

No doubt the story of my personal journey, which spanned three generations through the education system, might have remained just that, personal and private, had I not encountered Foucault in one of my first courses for a master of education degree. Even though I had great difficulty unravelling his obscure prose, for some reason it struck a resounding chord deep within me, and in the beginning it both puzzled and annoyed me. After all, what could a conventional wife, mother, grandmother, church-going senior citizen such as myself, who has always accepted the way things are, who has never thought "outside the box" have in common with a borderline anarchist, nihilist and nonconformist *par excellence* like Foucault, who appeared to thrive on challenge, confrontation and conflict? A more improbable alliance would be hard to conceptualize, since a more unlikely candidate than myself to defy the status quo can hardly be imagined. Yet I felt myself drawn to read more and more of his work. As I struggled to understand Foucault's unconventional use of such terms as *subject, regimes of truth, genealogy, discourse* and *normalization,* I felt at times that I was translating a foreign language. I was also becoming increasingly troubled by my growing conviction that he was speaking to me — was urging me to stand up for my beliefs. Beyond the fact that I lack the courage to speak out in public, I have always been told that it is useless to criticize unless one can offer an alternative solution. But, to my surprise, Foucault disagrees with that premise:

> Under no circumstances should one pay attention to those who tell you "Don't criticize, since you're not capable of carrying out a reform." That's ministerial cabinet talk. Critique doesn't have to be the premise of a deduction that concludes: This then is what needs to be done. It should be an instrument for those who fight, those who resist and refuse what is. Its use should be in processes of conflict and confrontation, essays in refusal. It doesn't have to lay down the law for the law. It isn't a stage in programming. It is a challenge directed to what is. (1987: 114)

Reading and accepting that advice marked the gradual beginning of the end of my resistance to Foucault, but I still had reservations. Was he actually proposing that people have a right, a duty, to speak out against a perceived injustice, or against any tenet of society with which they disagreed? I certainly felt that an injustice had been done to my grandson, but what could I be expected to do? Nothing, I hoped. Yet much of what he wrote and said was beginning to resonate within me, such as his belief in the need to have curiosity about our world because it evokes "a readiness to find what surrounds us strange and odd; a certain determination to throw off familiar ways of thought and to look at the same things in a different way"(xxi). That is exactly what I had to do as I grappled with his unique use of vocabulary.

The term *normalization* as used by Foucault refers, I understood, to society's attempts to get people to think and act a certain way, which those in authority consider to be the correct way.

By the *subject* I soon realized Foucault means a human being, an individual, and he devotes much of his writing to explaining the many ways that human beings are turned into subjects. His perception of the subject is not that of a pre-given, fixed entity. Foucault views the subject as a form rather than a substance, a form which is constituted by practices on itself. Yet these practices are not invented by the self; they are "models he finds in his culture and are proposed, suggested, imposed on him by his culture, his society, and his social group" (1997: 291). At first I was skeptical of this suggestion, but as I pondered it, I came to the conclusion that he is right. I am indeed mainly a product of the culture in which I was raised. Like Tennyson's *Ulysses* (1898: 88), "I am a part of all that I have met."

Foucault's understanding of the term *genealogy* differs slightly from the accepted sense of that word. Rather than seeing genealogy as a way of tracing the history of a person, he uses genealogy to trace the history of *ideas* from the past up to the present.

And for Foucault, *discourse* is much more than language, spoken or written. It also includes what can be thought, as well as who can speak, where and when and with what authority. He asserts that it is through discourse that the guidelines for truth are established.

But Foucault's insight about *truth* was the most important revelation of all, turning my ideas upsidedown:

> Truth is a thing of this world: it is produced under multiple forms of constraint. And it induces regular effects of power. Each society has its regime of truth, its general politics of truth: that is the types of discourse which it accepts and makes function as true. (1980: 133)

Was Foucault also suggesting that what we perceive to be the truth is not necessarily carved in stone but may have shifting and unstable origins?

That society constructs what he calls regimes of truth, a set of beliefs, to suit its particular needs at a particular time and, that as these needs change, truth can also change? That practices change according to who has power? I had to concede that is precisely what he is suggesting.

Then another paragraph jumped out at me:

> It seems to me... that the real political task in a society such as ours is to criticize the working of institutions which appear to be both neutral and independent; to criticize them in such a manner that the political violence which has always exercised itself obscurely through them will be unmasked, so that one can fight them. (Foucault, cited in Rabinow 1984: 6)

And like St. Paul at Damascus I finally saw the light. I became a disciple of Michel Foucault. I understood his message. We do not have to accept blindly every precept of our society as fixed and unchanging truth. It is the right and perhaps even the duty of every citizen to question, to confront and to challenge any rule or regulation of any institution in society which contributes to the subjugation of the individual. I now believe that labelling children ADHD can harm them. I would not stand idly by if I saw someone physically abusing a child; therefore I cannot stand by while children are emotionally abused, which can happen when they are labelled through psychological and educational processes of classification and categorization. So now I will pick up the gauntlet Foucault has thrown down for me. I will criticize the system. I will attempt to "unmask" the pain that schools inflict on children by labeling them ADHD. It may not be possible to bring about change, but I should, at least, create an awareness of this damaging practice. Maybe it will "contribute to changing certain things in people's ways of perceiving and doing things, to participate in this difficult displacement of forms of sensibility and thresholds of tolerance" (Foucault 1987: 112). At the very least, my criticism should be useful "as an instrument of struggle, with which the critic seeks to change, if only for the moment, the balance of power in the present regime of truth" (Baynes, Bohman and McCarthy 1987: 98). Foucault will assist. I will use one of his tools, genealogy, to challenge the truth of ADHD. I will expose it as simply one of the "regimes of truth" manufactured by society, in this case, one in which children are made objects in the school system through testing and labelling, then "normalized" into becoming docile beings, often through medication.

Following my story, I provide a methodological, theoretical and deconstructive analysis relating to ADHD. I look at ADHD through a Foucauldian lens.

Chapter One

THE NARRATIVE

Marion

I was born on a farm on Prince Edward Island during the Depression, a dreamy, shy, introspective child, the fourth of five children in an Irish-Catholic household, where the male species ruled supreme and authority was never questioned. During my first years of formal education, I attended a one-room country school, which, I have to say, was a very positive experience for me. Over four hundred of these buildings dotted the landscape of Prince Edward Island at that time. Naturally, there were drawbacks to this type of schooling. There could be about thirty children in ten different grades, so the one teacher had little time to spend with individual students who might be experiencing problems understanding particular concepts. But there were advantages as well. Children learned to work independently and cooperatively, helping each other and learning from each other. There were many levels of learning in that one-room classroom. As the teacher taught a lesson to each grade, every student in the classroom was able to benefit from that instruction, and so children were able to advance at their own rate in a way that may not be possible in today's one-grade classroom. I loved the atmosphere and eagerly absorbed every bit of knowledge gleaned by watching and listening to the older grades. Consequently, I completed eight grades in five years. After I had completed grade eight, I moved on from the one-room school. During my high school years I was taught by the Sisters of St. Martha, which was another positive experience. It goes without saying that *their* authority was never questioned. These women were dedicated to their craft, and, being such a willing and eager student, I blossomed under their supervision. My grade eleven teacher, in particular, inspired within me a love of literature, which has never been extinguished. Under her guidance I devoured volumes of literary works, never once questioning the authority of the author. In that era, students were not encouraged to question or to offer their opinion, but to regurgitate information, and that suited me perfectly. I was never one to speak up or to speak out, although some students did. I loved every minute of my classes and was sorry when it seemed as if my love affair with learning would end with my grade eleven graduation. At that time, grade eleven students on Prince Edward Island could attain university matriculation by following the Maritime Board curriculum and writing the Board examinations.

Unfortunately, although I harboured a secret dream of going on to university, that aspiration was destined to remain just a dream for many years.

For a woman growing up on Prince Edward Island during the forties and fifties, life was restricted and opportunities were limited. She had the choice of becoming a teacher, nurse or secretary, and those were considered interim occupations only, since the ultimate career was that of wife and mother. Working after motherhood was frowned upon except in cases of absolute necessity. There were no daycares on Prince Edward Island during that era. A university education was not forbidden but was not exactly encouraged. The first woman to graduate from St. Dunstan's (where the University of Prince Edward Island now stands) only did so in 1941, and she later became my much loved and aforementioned grade eleven teacher. My father, although or perhaps because he had very little formal schooling, was a firm believer in education for both men and women, but money was scarce, and there did not seem to be any bursaries or scholarships for women at that time. Boys' education was given priority, because it was felt that they would need it to earn the family's living, whereas girls would not need a university degree to change diapers or peel potatoes. Never one to challenge the status quo, I abandoned my dream of going to St. Dunstan's and dutifully followed my two sisters into the teaching profession.

At that time, to get a teacher's licence, all that was required after high school graduation was one year of teacher training at Prince of Wales College and Normal School, now the site of Holland College, Charlottetown Centre. Students could negotiate a loan from the Department of Education and also receive a bursary if they agreed to teach for two years in Prince Edward schools after receiving their licence. Both government and students benefited from this arrangement. Since teachers were scarce, the government was able to induce more students into the teacher-training program with the financial incentive, and since money was scarce, students were able to finance their training without putting undue strain on the family budget. This was what I did, and I began my teaching career in a little one-room school with nineteen pupils, grades one to ten. I discovered that I loved the children and really enjoyed teaching. I felt that I learned as much as the children. Teachers in those little country schools scattered over the Prince Edward Island countryside in the days before consolidation had a fair degree of autonomy. They were hired by a local board of three trustees, usually men, although the secretary could be a woman, who seldom interfered with the daily running of the school. In many cases trustees' only contribution was the supplement they paid the teachers to augment the not-too-generous salary received from the Department of Education. The money for this supplement came from the taxes paid by the residents of the school district and collected by the trustees. The Department of Education made available, in each school, a curriculum guide, which outlined in fairly general terms what a child was expected to master in each grade, and sent a person with the formidable title of School Inspector out to each school at least once a year to administer tests in math and English to the children. The Inspector was anticipated with a certain degree of trepidation by most teachers, as their teaching reputation hinged on the success of the pupils in these tests. As the same tests were given to students of schools which had two rooms, where the teacher only had half as many grades to teach, it was hardly a fair assessment. Once that visit was over, teacher and pupils breathed a sigh of relief and got on with the business of learning. There were meagre resources in the classroom besides a few books, a chalkboard, a globe and a map of Canada. Books could be borrowed from the Provincial Library. So the teacher had to be both resourceful and innovative. Physical training (known as PT) was taught on the playground, mostly with balls, bats and skipping ropes. Drama and music were introduced into the curriculum during the annual Christmas and end-of-year concerts. Children learned about leadership and also about caring for others through Red Cross meetings, which were conducted by the students monthly, usually on Fridays. Science and nature study were subjects which were sometimes taught outdoors through active participation. Pupils learned about native trees and plants by collecting leaves and wildflowers and taking walks through the countryside to observe the changing seasons and the habits and habitat of the wild animals. My experience in a country school showed me that learning involved more than sitting and listening and that teaching involved more than just standing in front of a class talking, that children learn more easily when they are actively engaged. This knowledge proved valuable to me in later years when I was raising my own children. I taught for only a few years and then at the age of twenty, married and moved on to a new stage in my life.

Marriage and Children

My husband had chosen to pursue a career in the Royal Canadian Air Force, and I soon discovered that, once again, I had moved into a world of male supremacy. There were no female mechanics, pilots, firefighters or navigators, but there were female nurses, clerical staff and cleaners. I found myself immersed in a patriarchal culture where authority emanated from the top down, and to question that authority was considered tantamount to treason. The motto of the Armed Forces was certainly not "women and children first." In fact, it was quite the reverse. Men and their needs were always paramount. A wife's role was to look after her husband and children and to provide a stable home life in whatever part of the world she found herself, due to her husband's postings.

She was expected to take on all parental responsibilities during her husband's frequent absences in the line of duty and never jeopardize her husband's career or opportunity for advancement by openly criticizing the upper echelons. And there were no support systems in place for families as there are today. A wife was on her own, usually far away from her own people. Again, I did exactly what I was supposed to do and never questioned the status quo. In the early years I actually enjoyed moving around and seeing different parts of the world. Soon after our marriage, my husband was posted to Europe to serve with the NATO (North American Treaty Organization) forces for three years. He was stationed in northeastern France at a Canadian Air Force base. It had living quarters for personnel, but since he was just beginning his career, he had not acquired enough points to entitle us to get an apartment immediately, so we lived off-base, at first in Belgium in the little village of St. Leger. We were quite happy about that as it gave us the opportunity to experience another culture and another language. The Belgian people were very happy to accommodate the Canadians because of the economic boost as well as the good reputation Canadians had abroad. We rented the upstairs of a dwelling from a family who lived on the first floor and also ran a small grocery there. There were other Canadian families living in the area, but at first we were completely on our own in a French-speaking community. We were living in this small village when our first child was born, changing our lives forever. Since we were both next to the youngest in our families, we had very little experience with babies or toddlers, but, undaunted, we plunged blissfully and blindly into that exciting world known as parenthood, and, thus, a new stage in our lives commenced.

Impending motherhood introduced me to many new experiences within and outside of this patriarchal culture to which I now belonged, the most immediate being that of prenatal care as administered by the Air Force authorities. On most Air Force bases within Canada, with the possible exception of those in "isolation," medical services were available to personnel only. Wives and children, known as *dependents,* looked to civilian doctors in the nearest town for their healthcare. However, on bases outside of Canada, healthcare was provided for both personnel and their dependents. And that included prenatal care, which was a far cry from what was offered in civilian life. The Air Force, as I remember it, was not geared to the individual. Everything was done collectively and impersonally. So every Tuesday all expectant mothers gathered at the hospital, a drab, rambling, one-storey structure, to participate in a ritual known as the "maternity parade." They were examined by whichever doctor was on duty that day. Having one's own doctor was not an option. Several physicians, most of whom were also members of the Air Force, were posted to the base to attend to the health requirements of the service personnel. At overseas bases their duties also included providing prenatal, delivery and postnatal care to the wives of the servicemen. As I remember they worked eight-hour shifts like almost everybody at the hospital, so a mother-to-be would not necessarily see the same doctor twice in a row, and for her delivery, might have a doctor whom she had never seen before. It was impersonal to the point of being almost dehumanizing. It was only in retrospect that I saw it in this way. At the time, without any prior experience of this phenomenon, I accepted it simply as "the way things were." When I needed prenatal care back in Canada some years later, I was astonished at the level of interest and concern for my well being shown by my doctor before, during and after delivery. However, that was far in the future, so, for the weeks leading up to the birth, I saw all four doctors in turn and actually managed to establish a rapport with one of them, who, unhappily for me, was not on duty when I arrived at the hospital for the birth.

Larry

My first child was born on a beautiful spring afternoon in 1957, without benefit of anesthetic and, unfortunately, without benefit of natural childbirth training. Obviously the Air Force believed that all that was necessary was a stiff upper lip. It was Mother's Day in France, which I thought most appropriate. Over a period of more than twenty-four hours I was assisted by three different doctors who were working three different shifts. After so many years, the details are, mercifully, quite hazy. I do remember taking one horrified look at the newborn, who to my mind did not resemble anything human since I had never seen a newborn, before he was whisked off to the nursery. The concept of bonding between mother and child had not been conceived, so new mothers only saw their babies for about twenty minutes every four hours, to bottle feed them, during the day, but they remained in the nursery from ten o'clock at night until six o'clock in the morning. This was standard procedure in most hospitals at the time. Breastfeeding was definitely discouraged. Babies were fed formula from a bottle. There was not much opportunity to learn how to look after a new baby, and little instruction was provided for first time mothers. A doctor would answer a question if asked, but not many new mothers knew what to ask. I was in hospital for eight days, which was the norm, where postnatal care, with the exception of a quick visit by the doctor on duty doing his daily rounds, was provided by female personnel who were known as "Med A's" (medical assistants). Since these assistants, like the doctors, were used to looking after men, they were famous neither for their sensitivity toward emotional new mothers nor for their nurturing qualities. Quite frankly, I was terrified of them, and, although I was apprehensive about my ability to provide adequate care for this little human being now entrusted to my care, it was with considerable relief that I left the hospital with my husband and baby son, armed with enough formula for two feedings and the recipe for making more. And so the motherhood saga, which has no end, began, culminating in the telling of this story. Fortunately, I did not know then that the job description for motherhood included the phrase "for the rest of your life." In some ways ignorance is indeed bliss.

Looking back and realizing the depth of my ignorance about babies, I marvel at the fact that our child survived infancy. I did not even know how to change a diaper. And that was the least of the things I did not know. As I left the hospital that beautiful day in early June, I was unaware that it would be the last time for at least three months that I would have time to notice the weather. I was certain of only two facts concerning babies. Their heads were very fragile so I must be careful never to drop my son, and babies were very susceptible to germs, so I must be vigilant about sterilizing bottles, nipples and all other formula equipment. My only source of information was a book called *The Canadian Mother and Child,* edited, I believe, by a male doctor. After a couple of weeks I threw it away as the information it contained bore absolutely no resemblance to my situation. The book explained how newborn babies sleep most of the time, only waking every four hours for nourishment, exactly four ounces, burping and then going back to sleep. It never mentioned babies who drank only two ounces, refused to burp, then threw up over everybody and everything, cried constantly and absolutely never, ever slept. Which meant their parents did not sleep either. Life became an endless nightmare of staggering around in a fog of exhaustion, sterilizing bottles, making formula and washing diapers, as there were no disposable diapers, punctuated always by the howls of an unhappy baby. I had no one to whom I could turn for help or advice. My family was thousands of miles away. There were Canadian families in the area, but we had no chance to really get to know them, and I think I would have been too proud to confess how inadequate I felt. My Belgian landlady was very kind but there was the language barrier. As well, her method of stopping the baby's cries was to feed him spoonfuls of sugar, at which even I, ignorant and desperate as I was, drew the line. My husband was extremely helpful when he was home. He seemed to have a knack for soothing the baby. He took a week's leave and then gratefully went back to work but helped as much as he could. It did not make us feel any better to hear about the baby of one of his fellow workers who was sleeping all night and drinking eight ounces at a feeding at the age of one month. We decided the father was being untruthful since our son had yet to sleep fifteen minutes night *or* day, drank only about a half ounce at a feeding and then, somehow, appeared to throw up eight. But we were young, healthy and optimistic and decided that, since this was the reality of life with a baby, we would adapt. And we did. By night, we took turns sleeping, and, if by chance Larry allowed himself to doze off, we both immediately collapsed as well. By day, I carried him around on my hip. To this day, I can do most household chores with one hand — my legacy from Larry. He and I enjoyed what I would best describe as a master-slave relationship, and emancipation seemed far in the future those first few months. He was either demanding to be fed, to be changed, to be burped or to be carried, and I complied. He appeared to fight sleep at every turn. Memory can be faulty, but I am fairly sure I read the lengthy novel *Gone with the Wind* in its entirety while trying to get him to sleep during one particularly difficult period when my husband was away. I used to say that when he graduated from high school he still had not slept through the night. In spite of everything, Larry appeared to flourish and actually began to gain a little weight. He was a beautiful baby with big blue eyes and blond hair. However, he looked very puny beside the huge Belgian babies when I started taking him to the village clinic to be checked and weighed by the Belgian doctor, who would weigh one of these enormously fat babies and then crossly demand of the mother, *"Qu'est ce que vous le nourrissez?"* When it was my turn, he would take one look at Larry, then growl *"Le nourrissez-vous?"* I did not blame him for asking. But I was not worried unduly about Larry's weight because there was not the obsession with "normal" weight and height and development that came into being by the time my grandchildren were being raised. Happily, I had never heard of percentiles.

When Larry was nearly two months old, we bought a car and, discovered, quite by chance, that the movement of the car put him to sleep. That revelation transformed our lives. Our every spare moment after that was spent traversing the roads of not only Belgium but France, Holland and Luxembourg as well. It is no wonder that, to this day, Larry loves to travel. Gradually, he was turning into a happy baby but one who felt sleeping was a waste of time. He was always alert and active and loved looking at books and pictures and grabbing at anything within his reach. Then he started to crawl. After that we hardly had time to eat. Soon he was standing up, taking unsteady steps, then walking. Actually, after the first few days, he never walked but ran. And we ran after him. He was curious and energetic, and very, very fast. We took our eyes off him at our peril. He was always struggling to be free — to get out of my arms, to get out of his crib, to get out the door — always wanting to go one step farther than could be allowed within the limits of safety. He loved to run through our landlady's garden, trampling her strawberries and cramming them into his mouth. Since she was a very thrifty lady, this did not please her and she would scold, *"Non, non Larry! Méchant garçon! Oh, il est méchant! Méchant garçon!"* He began to think that *Méchant Garçon* was his name. But she loved him like a grandmother and spent countless hours amusing him while I tried to do my household chores. It was out of the question to attempt any housework when Larry was awake. And he was awake a great percentage of the time. Since we had no experience and were living far from relatives and friends who might have enlightened us, we assumed this was the way all young children were, until we made friends with another Canadian couple who lived in the next village and had a child the same age. When we visited them one Sunday afternoon, the boy was sitting on the floor placidly playing with blocks, and the parents were reading. I was absolutely astounded. I burst out to my husband, "Look! He's awake and they're sitting down!" They were amazed at my amazement. This, to them, was perfectly normal behaviour. Secretly we believed there was something wrong with their child. To us, Larry was the one exhibiting "normal" behaviour.

He started to talk quite early and his first sentence was in French, *"Écoute le train."* This was due in part to the landlady's coaching and in part to the fact that we lived near a railway station. With the acquisition of language, a whole new world opened up for him and presented an additional challenge for us. Although his first speech was in French, Larry soon mastered the English language, which meant that we also had to become more versatile. Now, while we were chasing him, we were also answering his questions. And he could talk as fast as he could run. He was very curious about everything, and I was determined to answer always as truthfully and completely as I could. It seemed to me, as a child, that children were talked *about* and never *to* and that absolutely no one ever listened to them. I disagreed vehemently with that old belief that children should be seen and not heard. The way I have always understood it is that they ask because they want to know. So I responded patiently to endless rounds of "Why?" and "How come?" It was easier to answer questions than it was to cope with two of his favourite sayings, which were "No" and "I don't want to." I heard those a lot. Even at the tender age of two he didn't want his freedom to make his own choices restricted in any way.

After almost two years of living in Belgium, we moved into the Air Force married quarters situated in Longuyon, France, not far from the Belgian border. We were expecting our second child, and our apartment now seemed cramped and inconvenient. As well, it did not have central heating, and I minded the damp winters. Married quarters consisted of seven large, white, four-storied buildings imaginatively labelled A, B, C, D, E, F and G. We took up residence on the third floor of G Building. There were lots of children for Larry to play with and lots of young mothers like myself. In February 1959, our second son was born, at the same hospital where Larry's birth had taken place twenty-one months previously and with the same level of impersonal care. This time, at least, I knew what to expect. And to say that Larry was not happy with this new addition to our household is a vast understatement! Children were not allowed visiting privileges at the hospital, so my husband brought him to the window to look into my room. Unfortunately, it was feeding time for the babies. I can still see the look of absolute betrayal in his eyes as he saw the new baby with me. Then he shifted his gaze, looked beyond me and refused to look my way again. When I brought what he feared was his replacement home with me, I paid dearly for my perfidy. He would have nothing to do with me or this usurper and concentrated all his efforts on making life miserable for us both. Whenever I was busy with the baby, he would occupy himself ransacking the fridge, throwing stuff into the toilet or hurling the baby's things out the door. When the baby cried, Larry would drop things into his open mouth. Many times I narrowly saved Allan from choking. He would not call Allan by name, referring to him simply as "that baby" and hoping, I suppose, that he would disappear. He continued in that vein even after our third child was born, calling his two siblings "old baby" and "new baby." But he got over it eventually and became a kind and caring big brother. In this case, the old adage "A poor start makes a good finish," proved true. However, that was far in the future. In the weeks following Allan's arrival there was no sign of that kindness or caring. Again, for me, it was a question of survival. And I thought I was busy before! At least I had no time for postpartum depression, if such a concept had existed then. And to my great joy, Allan slept through the night before he was a month old.

We returned to Canada in February 1960, just before Larry was three and on Allan's first birthday. Eight days on an ocean liner may sound like heaven to those who have never crossed the Atlantic in February, four months pregnant, with a baby just learning to walk and a very active toddler. The reality was far from heavenly. Our arrival on Prince Edward Island was Larry's first opportunity to meet with aunts, uncles, grandparents and cousins. They were delighted. He was less so. To him they were annoying strangers who were forever trying to kiss him. "No the hug," he would scream and struggle to get away. We spent two months with family on P.E.I., then moved on to Ontario, where my husband was posted. We settled in an old farmhouse in the country, with few neighbours, which proved to be the best living quarters we could find at short notice. That was a difficult adjustment for Larry. I had occasion then to observe how hard it is for children who are old enough to notice, but too young to understand, to part with all things familiar and accept new surroundings and new people. Larry looked everywhere for those white apartment buildings and his little friends and would ask piteously, "Mommy, where's home? Where did home go?" This went on for two or three months.

In July 1960, our third child was born, a girl, who also slept through the night, which continued to be a source of wonder to me. When Larry was four, we moved into the city, to a two-storey brick house with a big back yard, near schools and playgrounds but situated on a busy street. This meant that, due to my tendency to worry about his safety, Larry could not have the independence he craved, such as going by himself to the playground or visiting children a few streets away. And at this age he needed more stimulation than I could provide easily with two younger children. There was not the array of organized activities for preschoolers that there is today. Where we lived, at any rate, children had to be school age to participate in any organized activity. I made a great effort to do interesting things. We went to the library, which he loved, and took part in story hour. We went to the park. We went sliding in winter and wading in the river in summer. But he was sometimes bored, and when Larry was bored, watch out! His siblings were at risk. Throughout his childhood, I learned to avoid these potentially hazardous situations by hastily inventing and presenting intellectually stimulating activities. At mealtimes we would play our version of Trivial Pursuit, long before the actual game was invented. On our long and tiring drive from Ontario to Prince Edward Island each summer, we would try to count the Thousand Islands in the St. Lawrence River. In dozens of ways I learned to forestall trouble. Larry taught us to be proactive rather than reactive. That lesson served me in good stead throughout my life. And all the children benefited from these intellectual exercises. But back when he was an active four-year-old, it wasn't always easy to keep him amused. One day in October he climbed to the top of the swing set, fell and broke his wrist. He spent a week in hospital, which was traumatic for him, as visiting hours were only two hours a day and young children weren't allowed to visit at all. And the worst indignity of all, he was confined to a crib! On Christmas Eve, the day after he got the cast off, he fell off his tricycle in the basement and broke his wrist again. 1961 was a year to forget.

The next year, however, was a year to remember. Larry was five years old and ready to venture out into the world. He started in kindergarten. I can still remember that first day. The two of us had waited a long time for this. We were both smiling, while all around us children were wailing and clinging to their mothers. Mothers were weeping and clutching their children. Larry was dumbfounded at this behaviour, and, I must confess, so was I. He kept exclaiming, "But what are they crying for, Mom?" He could not understand why anyone would cry over a step toward independence and freedom. It was one of the happiest days of his short life. I must admit that I was fairly happy too. I would have two hours every day to sit down and catch my breath, without having to deal with such issues as his brother being tied to a tree or his sister being locked in a closet.

Kindergarten was a wonderful experience. It was play-based, and Larry loved to play. Now his horizons had broadened considerably. There were opportunities to make new friends at the kindergarten. There were birthday parties to attend and invitations to play at friends' homes. There were school activities, such as the Christmas concert, in which he enthusiastically participated. His teacher was extremely pleased with him because he liked to sing and he liked to perform, and he did both with great zest. As well, she felt he was more advanced than most of the others and suggested that he move into a class of children who were beginning to read. Naturally we were delighted and agreed. But if I had that decision to make again, recognizing how important play was to him, I would never have consented. He had years to do the academic stuff but not nearly enough time to play. Sadly, hindsight, instead of foresight, is nearly always twenty-twenty. He got along well, however, except with printing, which he did not like because it was repetitive and, therefore, boring. That led to a familiar refrain, which we heard from every teacher down through the years. "Larry is clever but very careless with his written work." To this day his writing is almost illegible.

Those early years of schooling flew by swiftly and smoothly. Larry excelled in all areas except printing, since he was always in a rush to finish so he could play. He had no complaints about school, but recess was always his favourite time. The teachers were encouraging and supportive, noting always his great natural ability, while urging him to slow down and take more pride in his work. They also recognized that it was sometimes hard for him to sit still. Outside of school, his horizons had broadened even more. There were several areas now into which he could channel his boundless energy. When he was seven, he enrolled in swimming lessons and started playing hockey, two sports which he enjoys to this day. He loved all sports, but there was not the bewildering array from which to choose that there is nowadays. And they were affordable for everybody. There was hockey in winter, baseball in summer, football in fall, swimming all year round. Games were only once or twice a week and never before dawn, as is often the case today. So there was lots of time for unstructured play, such as marbles, building forts, riding bikes and the inevitable road hockey. A backyard rink provided hours of entertainment. The world was not such a dangerous place for children during the sixties, so they could roam around more freely. At the age of nine, Larry could travel all over the city. All in all it was a happy time for everyone, since he did not crave any more freedom than we were willing to grant. Our fourth child was born, a third boy, and for the first time Larry was delighted to be a big brother.

In 1966, when Larry was in grade four, my husband was transferred to Prince Edward Island. We were all happy to be coming home. This was not a difficult move for the children, because we had travelled home each summer and they had lots of cousins to see. Again, we were not immediately eligible for military housing, so, briefly, we moved into an old farmhouse in rural Prince Edward Island, and the children attended a one-room country school, housing grades one to six, for a short period of time. These schools disappeared in the early seventies when a massive restructuring of education took place in this province. The children absolutely loved the atmosphere of the one-room school and were sorry to leave it when we were eventually allotted a house in a military subdivision in Summerside. Larry made the transition smoothly. He continued to excel academically and continued to be careless in his work. The teachers recognized that he was very bright, that he often had difficulty sitting still and that he would sometimes try to distract his classmates. They viewed him as a child with a great deal of potential and a great deal of energy. In grade six, he asked to go to the bathroom so often that the new, young teacher advised us to get his kidneys checked, in case there was a problem; which we did, and there wasn't. We explained that this was his way of dealing with periods of long inactivity. She saw it as her problem rather than his and allowed him some leeway. He was demonstrating his need to make his own choices in other little ways. One of these concerned his participation in the music festival. Music teachers had frequently praised his singing ability, and, therefore, he was always entered in the singing competition in the music festival. As he got older he didn't want to do it, but I would override his decision and fill in the form to register him. Finally he took matters into his own hands. He stood on the stage, while I sat proudly in the audience, sang a few bars and then stopped. He said he had forgotten the lyrics. Needless to say, he won that round, and singing competitively was dropped from his agenda.

Before I knew it Larry was in junior high. He liked the extra freedom and the extra movement, such as going from classroom to classroom for different subjects. And he liked the classes too. His home-room teacher gave him extra, more challenging reading and writing assignments, and he responded well. Also, we were allowing him to go on little excursions with his friends, bowling or to movies. Our youngest daughter, a fifth child, was born that year, and our house became very crowded. We had an opportunity to buy a farmhouse, without any farm, in the community where we had grown up, so before I knew it, I was back living in an old, cold farmhouse. In spite of my personal feelings about the move, I realized that country living would be good for the children, and, since the community was known for its high standards in education, I knew they would not suffer in that area. The younger children loved it, but at the age of thirteen, Larry found it harder to find his niche, although he settled easily into the school system and performed so well that he was selected "Student of the Year" in grade eight. But he preferred the faster pace of city life and the easy access to activities. In the country, he had to be driven wherever he needed to go, and he did not like that. He was moving into the adolescent stage, with a craving for independence, and we, as parents, were totally unprepared. Once more, as when he was born, we had arrived in unfamiliar and often hostile territory with no roadmap. The parenting skills we had so painfully acquired over the years no longer seemed applicable.

The sixties and seventies were not easy years for parents of teens. Rebellion was in the air. Freedom was the buzz word. All over North America young people were rebelling against what they perceived as bigotry and hypocrisy practised by authority figures. Those were the years made famous by the Freedom Riders in the United States, Le Front de libération du Québec, the flower children and the hippies. There were clashes between youth and authority on the street, on the university campus and in the home. Young people were "dropping out" in droves, hitchhiking all over the country, settling down in communes, doing their own thing. Conformity to the rules of the establishment was the cardinal sin. And, thanks to the advancement of communication technology, even little Prince Edward Island was not immune to this unrest. It was not only neophyte parents like ourselves who panicked over things as trivial as boys wearing long hair. When some enterprising individuals organized an outdoor rock concert in the early seventies, the good citizens of P.E.I., fearing perhaps that their island would become another Sodom or Gomorrah, raised such a public outcry that the provincial government passed a law forbidding public gatherings over a certain size, resulting in the scaling down of the concert to the extent that it was almost a non-event. This in turn garnered such scathing attacks on the government by liberal-minded individuals that it quietly rescinded the law a few weeks later. This then was the climate into which Larry entered his teenage years. It suited him. If there had been barricades on Prince Edward Island, he would have been at them.

He started high school in 1971 and graduated in 1975. The high school in this community included grades nine to twelve. These years, for Larry, were not an unqualified academic success. He had always loved to play, and now his social life took precedence over studying. Homework was something to be ignored, which drew the ire of some of his teachers. For the first time in his educational journey, I did not enjoy parent-teacher interviews, and I was at loss to understand what had happened. Probably his perfectly normal quest for independence, to be master of his own fate, the rigidity of the school administration and the general air of unrest in society all combined to alienate him from the school environment. High school was not his finest hour academically. He found many of the classes dull and uninspiring and some of the teachers critical and uncompromising. I learned from Larry that children do not forget perceived unfairness by a teacher and also that learning does not take place in a classroom where trust and acceptance are missing. Years later he was still smarting from remarks made by a teacher to the effect that he would never amount to anything because he was always putting his feet on the desk. Again, with the benefit of hindsight, I can see that we should have supported him more and the teachers and the system less. But we were still living in a world where the authority figure was always right, even though youth had begun to question that assumption. However, during those stressful times Larry always remained good-humoured, never moody, temperamental or disrespectful, unlike his nearest siblings — those two who had slept through the night. And there were redeeming factors at school too. There were teachers who sympathized with him, who recognized his ability, even though his marks did not reflect that ability, and whom he has not forgotten either.

I aged considerably during those four years, caused primarily by two factors: Larry's penchant for hitchhiking and his acquisition of a driver's licence at the age of sixteen. He loved the freedom that wheels provided and willingly worked on weekends to pay for his insurance. I spent my evenings praying for his safe return. Hitchhiking was a way of life for young people during those years and was comparatively safe. At age seventeen, having completed grade eleven, Larry felt the call of the open road and wanted to hitchhike to Ontario during the summer to visit his childhood friends. I was aghast. But he had an unexpected ally in the form of his heretofore authoritarian and unsympathetic father, who felt it would be a maturing experience and overrode my objections. I was sure I would never see him again. The fact that he returned safely and triumphantly renewed my faith in a God who must have a soft spot in his heart for uptight mothers.

High school graduation day came, and he did quite well, though not up to the level of his ability, and in September 1975, Larry was off to university, about which there had never been any question. Education has always been championed in our home. Books were plentiful and prominent. We took a keen interest in our children's progress in school and constantly advocated the joys of learning. Our home community, as well, is noted for promoting higher learning, which was one of the reasons I agreed to move back. It was one of the first rural areas on Prince Edward Island to establish a high school and boasts a high number of university graduates. That year, as usual, the majority of the high school graduates were going on to further study, and, no doubt, that had some influence on Larry's decision to attend the University of Prince Edward Island. He was even happier than the day he started to kindergarten. He was finally free to live his own life. We were happy for him too. Naturally we had regrets; we knew we had made mistakes in our parenting. Guilt seems to be a never-ending fact of life for many parents. There were things we would have done differently if we could have done them over again, but we felt Larry had the intelligence, ability, drive and confidence to excel in whatever he decided to do in life. And he did not betray our faith in him. It took him a while to adjust to the freedom associated with university life and to decide which path his career would follow. He graduated in 1980 and went on to postgraduate studies. Today he is a successful, productive and still very energetic member of society. Therefore, when our first grandson, Benjamin, was born (Larry's nephew), and he exhibited those similar traits of energy, intelligence, curiosity and enthusiasm for life, we were sure he would enjoy the same success, during his school days, that Larry had experienced. But, sadly, that was not to be. Times had changed, and so had the education system.

Ben

The world in 1985, when Ben's parents started raising their family, was far different from the one in which I had begun my parental journey almost thirty years previously. The turbulent sixties and seventies had left their mark on society. There were changes, both positive and negative, in the areas of family life, health and education, which were the areas in which I tended to be interested. The baby boomers had now become baby producers, and their values and expectations were slightly different from those of their parents. They had their own "regimes of truth." Research showed the importance of bonding between mother and child from the moment of birth and that one way to reinforce this bonding was through breastfeeding. In a surprising turnaround from the fifties, when formula was touted as the perfect food for babies, breast milk was now pronounced the ideal nourishment. At the same time, fathers became much more involved in childbirth, child rearing and the education of their children.

The social aspect of learning began to be emphasized. Baby boomers wanted their children to be successful in life, so they felt that preparation had to begin early. Daycare centres and nursery schools were established, not only to accommodate working families, but to provide opportunities for very young children to associate with and learn from their peers. Many schools, in Ontario especially, offered both junior and senior kindergarten. Organized activities began to be available for children at younger and younger ages; these included swimming lessons for babies, music lessons for tots, skating and hockey for children who were barely able to walk. Such emphasis was put on supervised activities that little time remained for old-fashioned, unstructured play.

Many changes were enacted in the education system, not all of them beneficial. Bigger was considered better. Bigger and bigger schools were built. Often this also meant bigger classes, which put more pressure on teachers, leaving them less opportunity to work with children on an individual basis. Some children suffered more than others from this new direction in education, and one of the trends which had the greatest effect on children was testing. Testing was one of the new practices I encountered when I rejoined the teaching profession.

In the late seventies, with three children in university, I re-entered the work force, but it was difficult to get a position in the public school system since consolidation of schools had resulted in a surplus of teachers. However, the importance of early childhood education had begun to be recognized on Prince Edward Island, so I soon gained employment as a teacher in a privately run kindergarten. I worked with children who would be entering grade one the following year, and that is when I became aware that extensive testing of children had been introduced into the public school system, with the result that children were being grouped into categories, supposedly for their benefit. Labels such as "developmentally delayed," "slow learner," "gifted" and "learning disabled" were being bandied about. I was never comfortable with this process of labelling children. I believed in the individual worth of every child and maintained that children should be allowed to develop at their own rate without being categorized. To my mind, there is no one way to learn, no one age to learn, no one style of learning. Then in the eighties, when many educators began jumping on the bandwagon of a new phenomenon known as attention deficit hyperactivity disorder (ADHD), I became increasingly concerned. It seemed to me that too many active, inquisitive, free-spirited children, children who exhibited almost the same characteristics that Larry had displayed, were now being tested, diagnosed, labelled ADHD and medicated. Many of these children were boys. It was almost an epidemic. During the nineties, the numbers of children thus labelled increased dramatically. In many cases, parents, feeling powerless and desperately wanting their children to succeed, were influenced by teachers, pediatricians and psychologists (considered to be the experts) into accepting the diagnosis ADHD and putting their child on medication. This was brought home to me in a very personal way when Ben entered the education system in 1991 and almost immediately fell victim to the ADHD labeling that was sweeping the country. I was appalled because there was no indication during his early years that he would have a problem succeeding academically. In fact, quite the reverse seemed more likely. I did not believe the diagnosis.

Born in Calgary in September 1985, the oldest of four boys, Ben was an alert and happy baby, who did not seem to require a lot of sleep. He spent his first Christmas with us here on Prince Edward Island when he was three months old. He was the first grandchild, the first nephew. The whole family adored him, fought over the right to hold him, reluctantly handing him to his mother only when it was time for him to nurse. The days of preparing formula were long gone, I noted thankfully. We were now in the era of breastfeeding and bonding. We hated to see him leave us when the holidays were over, but his parents had settled in Calgary, so that would be his home.

However, we resolved that distance would not rule out a close relationship with our grandson. In May 1986, I went to visit and wound up looking after Ben because his mother had an opportunity to begin a new job. He was nine months old, crawling, pulling himself up and walking around the furniture, always on the move. I felt as if the clock had been turned back twenty-eight years because he was so similar to my eldest son at that age, not at all in appearance, but in energy level, curiosity in the world around him and disinterest in sleep. It was as if he did not want to go to sleep in case he missed something. It was obvious that he was a very alert child. Even at the age of nine months, he had the same uncanny ability, as Larry'd had, to read people and to sense whom he could manipulate. But I had learned from Larry, the master of manipulation, the importance of being kind but firm and consistent. I established a routine with Ben. A long walk in the stroller looking at lots of interesting things was followed by lunch and a nap in his crib, where he was expected to go to sleep on his own. He was outraged the first day because he wanted to be rocked until he fell asleep. Rocking him to sleep was an exercise in frustration, I discovered, because the presence of another person stimulated him into wakefulness. He cried only the first day after being put in his crib. After that, each day, he went to sleep out of sheer boredom probably. When his parents tried my method on the weekend, he objected so vehemently that they ended up taking him out and rocking him for hours, while he gazed at me in triumph. We had to find a solution, because his mother was working and needed her rest, and I would soon be going home. We solved that problem by having his mother put him to bed and then go for a drive, while I stayed just outside his door. He howled lustily the first evening, expecting his mother to give in, but when she did not appear, he finally went to sleep. We did that for a few evenings until he accepted bedtime without rocking.

The next summer, 1987, I returned to Calgary for the months of July and August. A new baby was expected in September. Ben was almost two, talking, an inquisitive and active toddler who seldom walked but ran and appeared to be delighted with the world around him. He would race around the back yard, sniffing flowers and often yanking them out. Like Larry, he liked lots of stimulation and seldom played quietly alone. He was not at all shy, loved being around people, and so he was very happy when visitors came to the house or when we went shopping in the malls. We spent a pleasant summer together, going for walks, visiting the playground, looking at pictures and reading books. One of his favourite picture books was the Canadian Tire catalogue, which he took to bed with him. I kept a journal that summer, and on looking over it now, I see often the comment, "Ben is very clever." On Sundays, the whole family would pack a lunch and drive into the mountains, picnicking in the scenic parks. Ben loved driving in the car and thoroughly enjoyed the time spent in the outdoors. And so the summer flew by, until it was time for me to return to Prince Edward Island. Ben's brother was born in September, and, according to his parents, Ben was no happier than Larry had been when his first sibling appeared. The following year, Ben, his mother and year-old brother visited his maternal grandparents in New Brunswick and made a brief visit to Prince Edward Island. He was still full of energy, still happy to be traveling, still interested in everything, still not thrilled with his sibling.

In 1990, I spent the month of July in Calgary looking after the two boys. Ben was almost four and was registered in preschool for September. To my mind, he was ready for more interaction with his peers. There were no children of his age living nearby, and like Larry at that age, he needed more stimulation. We went to the library, which he enjoyed. We went to the playground, where he was delighted if there were children to watch or to join in play. He loved to play. He had an unerring sense of direction and could tell me the way home from almost any part of Calgary. His father brought home a small two-wheel bicycle for Ben, and before the afternoon was over he had learned to ride it. Again I saw the resemblance to Larry. Nothing was too hard for him to do if he was motivated. He was looking forward to preschool and being with children his own age, anticipating the new experiences and stimulating activities which preschool would certainly offer. I was certain he would love it and would benefit greatly from it. The reality was far different.

Since Ben was their oldest, his parents had limited knowledge of preschools in Alberta, which were mostly run by the private sector. They really didn't know what to look for, so depended on those with experience to advise them. The one they chose for Ben came highly recommended and was considered one of the best. Another decidedly favourable factor was that it was at a convenient location for the babysitter. And so with high hopes Ben began his educational journey, attending preschool two days a week. It may indeed have been the best for some children but definitely was not the best for Ben. It was also a forerunner of his experience in the school system. It was highly structured and rigidly run, very unusual for a preschool. Children were expected to listen attentively, obey immediately, stand quietly in line and never interrupt. Docility was valued much more than creativity, which was so different from Larry's experience. For a little boy who had trouble sitting still and who loved to play, it was a disaster. There were many high expectations of the children, involving activities which were not age appropriate. Ben's parents were not aware of this until much later, but they did notice the rapid waning of his enthusiasm for preschool. He even confided to his father that he thought his teacher was a witch. But the words of four-year-olds are not often taken seriously. It was only much later that they found out that Ben was scolded frequently for such trivialities as fidgeting during circle time, speaking out of turn or walking too fast in line. When I viewed a videotape they sent me of the end-of-year concert and graduation, I was horrified at what I saw and heard. First, members of the audience, which consisted mostly of parents, grandparents and siblings, were lectured on proper behaviour, siblings warned not to interrupt, parents reminded not to wave at their children. Then the performance began. It was *The Wizard of Oz*, a fairly ambitious project for four-year-olds. The props were realistic, and the costumes were authentic. Only the children looked unreal. They were like little robots, moving only when they were told, repeating only the lines that the teacher said first, doing exactly as they had been told. All but Ben, that is! The video shows him defiantly waving to his parents, who were of course mortified, perform-ing very reluctantly in his role of munchkin, which he did not want to be and disliked the costume, yawning prodigiously throughout the program, refusing to shake hands with the director when he received his diploma and running back to his place instead of walking sedately. In my opinion Ben was almost the only child who acted like a four-year-old, but he did not get a favourable report from the director, and, sadly, she half convinced his mother that he was not up to standard because he did not conform. However, the year was over, and we all felt that real school would be more challenging and interesting for him. It should have been. But for the most part, it turned into thirteen years of misery for Ben, years of feeling different, of feeling stupid, of feeling helpless and hopeless, like a puppet on a string, jerked this way and that by the experts in the field of child development, as they offered conflicting opinions on his academic ability. The ordeal ended on the final day of grade twelve, but the scars remain. This was very different from Larry's school experience. Could it have been, perhaps, in part, because developmental and educational psychology as regimes of truth had not gained a foothold in the schools in the sixties as they had in the eighties and nineties?

What happened at school to turn a fearless confident five-year-old into a self-hating, school-hating nineteen-year-old who never wanted to see the inside of another learning institution and who still cannot drive onto school property without having those old familiar feelings of stupidity and worthlessness wash over him? What happened was that he was labelled ADHD very soon after he entered the school system.

Unfortunately for Ben, his school was a very *traditional* type of school (traditional in the worst sense of the word). Children spent a lot of time sitting quietly and listening to the teacher, working at their desks. There was not much opportunity for creativity or thinking. And Ben liked to think for himself. He did not see why carrots had to be colored orange all the time anyway. He found it difficult to sit quietly for long periods of time doing repetitive and boring work such as colouring (being sure to stay inside the lines) and printing. He began to fidget, to leave his seat without permission and to become inattentive and unfocused.[1] This behaviour did not go unnoticed in this traditional classroom. His teacher expressed concern that he was not conforming to classroom rules, and believing that she recognized the symptoms of a serious problem, informed Ben's parents that she thought he had ADHD, suggesting that they make an appointment with a developmental pediatrician at the Alberta Children's Hospital. Ben was just six years old. The parents were very concerned, but, remembering the preschool teacher's assessment of him and feeling that these people were the experts, they made the appointment. They were told by the pediatrician that he was too young to be assessed, but from observing him, in her opinion, he was perfectly fine. She advised them to bring him back in a few years if there were any difficulties. The parents were relieved, but that was not the end of the problem. It was only the beginning because, from that moment on, Ben never stepped out from under the shadow of ADHD. Even though there had been no diagnosis, he was treated from then on as if there was something wrong with him. The assumption was that he had ADHD. The teachers were so critical that he began to believe he was not okay. He began to dislike school and everything he associated with it. The little boy who had loved to look at books did not want to read anymore. He often got into trouble because he would act impulsively, which reinforced the teacher's opinion that there was something wrong with him. Many times he was blamed for things he had not done. When a child has a certain label, that's what people tend to see. In grade two he was accused of something quite serious, which he denied. The teacher and principal tried to force him to admit it. The parents were called in. They felt that the teacher must be right and also tried to get him to admit it, which he refused to do. The incident affected him quite negatively. He became intimidated by school authorities and no longer trusted them. As well, he began to doubt himself and his abilities. School turned into one bad experience after another. Teachers complained to the parents about his inattentiveness, his refusal or inability to complete his work, his impulsivity. He was never ever praised and constantly criticized. And he was still only in grade four.

When Ben was nine years old, he and his younger brother travelled by plane, on their own, from Calgary to Halifax, changing planes in Toronto. We met them and took them to Prince Edward Island for the month of July. Many nine-year-olds could not have performed as capably and responsibly. I wished that his teachers could have seen him. I could see that Ben was changing. He seemed angry a lot of the time. We did not talk about school, because I sensed that he wanted to forget all about it. We just concentrated on seeing that the boys enjoyed themselves. Ben still liked to be active, so we obliged him. We swam at many different beaches, went sightseeing, visited relatives, picked berries. The boys worked in the garden with their grandfather and spent hours playing horseshoes with him. Ben was interested in everything and was particularly fascinated with the Confederation Bridge, which was under construction at the time. He loved to watch the big floating crane, the Svanen, transport the big supporting pillars from the construction yard to their proper place. He also could express himself very well. My opinion of him had not changed. I saw him as a bright and capable youngster but suspected that he did not see himself in that light, which broke my heart. The holiday was a wonderful experience for us all.

Back at school in September, things had not changed. He was in grade five. There were more complaints from the teachers. The school was slow getting an assessment done, so his parents had him assessed at a place outside the school system called The Reading Foundation. The report was inconclusive, but the process convinced him that he was somehow at fault. He began to call himself a loser. We visited Calgary that year, and it was plain that he was not happy at school and that the school was not happy with him. In grade seven, it was suggested that he be assessed once more, at the Children's Hospital. This time he was finally diagnosed as having ADHD, by a different developmental pediatrician than the one who had seen him a few years before, and prescribed Ritalin. It hurt his stomach, and he had trouble sleeping, so he was put on Dexedrin. When it bothered him in the same way, an anti-psychotic drug, Risperdal, was prescribed to counteract the side effects of the Dexedrin. When his parents realized that this drug had major side effects, they took him off everything. He was sent to yet another developmental pediatrician, who recommended that he go to a school at the Children's Hospital called the Dr. Gordon Townshend School, where he would be monitored for three weeks by a team of experts, consisting of a psychiatrist, a psychologist, a teacher and a case worker. To get there, he had to travel on a bus for people with disabilities, which he did not want to do. His mother says that experience really scarred him, almost totally shattering his self-esteem. He was thirteen, an age where the opinion of peers really matters. The consensus of the experts was that Ben had a non-verbal learning disability, that he had difficulty processing information. This time he was also diagnosed as having oppositional defiant disorder, along with ADHD, although not all four agreed on that. One of the four thought he was fine. They recommended that he attend a special needs school in the fall. Most time the experts held a consultation with Ben's parents they included Ben. He would listen to all this dialogue about himself, often not understanding it completely. One thing he did take from those meetings was that he was different, which seemed to indicate that he was deficient in some way.

In the summer of that year, 1999, Ben and his brother vacationed with us again on Prince Edward Island. The Confederation Bridge had been completed, and they were very excited to drive over it. They wanted to repeat every single thing they had done when they had been here before, and so we did. It was plain that Ben had problems with self-esteem and self-confidence, but he was not in the least inattentive or unfocused, but alert, interested and interesting. He was articulate and interacted well with all age groups. I wished that his teachers could see him, but I was very angry at what the school system was doing to him. Both boys enjoyed themselves and seemed reluctant to leave Prince Edward Island.

That fall he started at the special needs school for children labelled *learning disabled*. It was soon obvious that he did not belong. He was far too advanced and spent his time helping the other children. His parents removed him from that school and decided to put him back into his regular school. But they encountered some difficulty. The principal called them in for a meeting and suggested that Ben did not belong in a regular school. The parents had to appeal to the superintendent in order to get Ben reinstated. This assuredly did not make Ben's life any easier at school. He was constantly watched and jumped on for even minor mistakes. Many times he was humiliated in front of his class. His parents tried to find another school but were unable to. There was one bright spot during his last year there. One of his teachers got to know him and realized that he was quite capable of doing the work. And Ben responded favourably.

High school presented more problems. He was not allowed into the regular grade ten class because the administrator insisted that he had not completed the necessary requirements. He was assigned to a "special class," where there were teaching assistants. To Ben this was the worst indignity of all. He complained that the assistants treated them like idiots or babies, reading the material for them and "dumbing it down." This, no doubt, took place with the best of intentions. No one seemed to realize his learning potential. He felt humiliated. He began to skip school and hang out with people whom his parents felt would be a bad influence. He was drifting away from them, and they were worried sick. In desperation, they met with the administrator and persuaded him to let Ben into the regular grade eleven class on a trial basis. He had no difficulty though he took an extra year to fulfill the requirements because of his lost year in grade ten. Ben finished his grade twelve year in 2004, one credit short of graduation requirements, having been effectively turned off by the very system which should have introduced him to the joy of learning, "the only societal institution designed exclusively for children." To me this is a tragedy. But at least Ben did almost complete grade twelve and is in a good position to access higher learning should he ever recover from the painful experiences he suffered during his years in the education system. He endured mainly due to the fact that he had middle-class, educated parents who, though buffeted and broad-sided by the endless stream of professionals with their "expert" opinions, did have the capability, the confidence and the determination to negotiate the system and to fight for Ben's education rights. But what if Ben had come from a different background, a background where dropping out of school is seen as the only option for "problem" children? What if Ben had been from "the other side of the tracks," with parents who were too preoccupied with providing the basic necessities for their children to have the time, energy or knowledge to fight the system? What if Ben's parents had been too intimidated by the school authorities to push for Ben's reinstatement in regular classes? Then this story would have had a different ending because Ben would likely have dropped out of school long before grade twelve. And there are hundreds of *Bens* who are exactly in that position, children who drop out of school in grade nine or ten because they have been regarded and treated by educators as "problem children." Many of these children are boys. They have been tested, labelled, medicated, blamed and isolated from their peers. Every day in school has reinforced their belief that they are failures. Like Ben, their self-esteem is completely shattered. And, unlike Ben, they may have no one to fight for them. Their situation is far more disturbing. Theirs is the real tragedy. And so it is with the hope of possibly preventing another child from experiencing a similar fate that I have decided to relate my story.

Note

1.   In her book, *Foucault and Education* (2005: 3), Jardine explains that many children fall into this pattern of behaviour. She reminds us that "we too often see young children who are physically, mentally, and emotionally active — full of life, curiosity, wonder, creative ideas, questions, and deep feelings — enter school and become subdued once they become convinced that they must learn and be exactly what their teacher rewards them for learning and becoming. Once in school, children may not be allowed to be active when their body leads them to be, but only on the schedule that their teacher allows or on the school's schedule of gymnasium availability. Moreover, we name their body restlessness as 'misbehavior' and attempt to redirect such students through acts of discipline, punishment, redirection, labeling, categorizing, and so on."

Chapter Two

EXPLORING A LIFE,
ILLUMINATING A CULTURE

The main interest in life and work is to become someone else that you
were not in the beginning. (Foucault 1982: 10)

Autoethnography as a Form of Narrative

The telling of one's personal experience so that it may have wider social implications is known as autoethnography, a particular form of narrative research.
Funk and Wagnall's Dictionary (1955) provides one definition of narrative
as "an orderly continuous account of an event or series of events." Donald
Polkinghorne (1988), eminent psychologist and an influential advocate of
narrative, elaborates on that definition: "Narrative displays the significance
events have for one another" (13), and "recognizes the meaningfulness of
human experiences by noting how they function as parts in a whole" (36).
My story illustrates both the definition and Polkinghorne's interpretation. My
growing-up years, when my parents instilled in me the value of education and
when there was such a close connection between the home and the school,
gave me a profound respect for and love of learning and an understanding
of the way it shapes one's life. My experience had a decided impact on how I
reacted to both my son's and grandson's experiences with the education system. Therefore, my son's story and my grandson's story are part of my story.
Polkinghorne believes, furthermore, that "the stories we encounter carry
the values of our culture by providing positive models to emulate and negative models to avoid" (14). My story illustrates both positive and negative
influences in our education system. Ben's experience reveals that the present
system places a great value on conformity and discourages any learning style
that deviates from the norm.

In his endorsement of narrative, Polkinghorne enjoys the company of
several other notable scholars, such as Barthes and Duisit (1975), Bruner
(1990), Clandinin and Connolly (2000) and Ellis and Bochner (2000), all of
whom have written about the centrality of narrative in our lives. French literary
critic Roland Barthes explains that "the narratives of the world are without
number.... Narrative is present at all times, in all places, in all societies; the

history of narrative begins with the history of mankind; there does not exist, and never has existed, a people without narratives" (cited in Polkinghorne 1988: 14).

The Meaning and Purpose of Narrative

My narrative reflects Barthes' theory that "narratives perform significant functions. At the individual level, people have a narrative of their own lives which enables them to construe what they are and where they are headed. At the cultural level, narratives serve to give cohesion to shared beliefs and to transmit values" (cited in Polkinghorne 1988: 14).

Jerome Bruner (1915–), one of the best known American psychologists of the twentieth century and who has written many books on education, regards learning as a narrative-centred process. Bigge and Shermis (1999: 142) endorse Bruner's position concerning the importance of narrative, stating that "narrative — story telling — is one of the most ubiquitous and powerful forms of human communication and learning." My personal experience with narrative corroborates this. Storytelling has always been a big part of my life. It was through the stories my mother told about growing up in her native Ireland that I became acquainted with my heritage. It was through her "Sunday evening stories" that I learned about the customs, climate, history and fierce patriotism of the Irish people. Consequently, when I visited Ireland as a young woman of twenty-one, I did not feel like a "stranger in a strange land" but experienced an instant connection. I, in turn, passed these stories on to my children, who are now educating their children in the same way on family traditions and history. Stories have an impact on the listener. It is my hope that those who hear Ben's story will empathize with him, have a greater understanding of the problems caused by labelling practices and have a greater sympathy for the labelled, supporting the position of Clandinin and Connelly (2000: 18), who conclude that "narrative is the best way of representing and understanding experience."

Narrative, according to Ellis and Bochner (2000: 750), "is always a story about the past ... one selective story about what happened written from a particular point of view for a particular purpose." I agree with their observation. I tell my story from the perspective of a person informed about our education system, of a former teacher, of a mother but, first and foremost, from the perspective of a grandmother looking back through the years, reflecting particularly on the education system throughout three generations, wondering how this system which served herself and her son so well could have completely failed her grandson, and hoping that by the telling, people will become aware of the damage done to a child's psyche through this process of labelling. My son's story and that of my grandson are "sub-stories," but the story is told always from my perspective, and the reflections are mine, as I try to tell it as truthfully and as accurately as I can without claiming to have discovered any universal truth. To quote Foucault: "I believe too much in truth not to suppose that there are different truths and different ways of speaking the truth" (cited in Tamboukou and Ball 2003: 14). I am saying simply that this is the way events in my life unfolded down through the years, and these are my thoughts and feelings about that process. Therefore, it is a subjective account, as autoethnography is meant to be. As Ellis and Bochner (2000: 752) remind us:

> Events in the past are always interpreted from our current position. Yet that doesn't mean there's no value in trying to disentangle now from then, as long as you realize it's not a project you'll ever complete or get completely right.

Britzman (2000: 38) suggests:

> Writing ethnography, as a practice of narration, is not about capturing the real already out there. It is about constructing particular versions of truth, questioning how regimes of truth become neutralized as knowledge, and thus pushing the sensibilities of readers in new directions.

In my story, I question the manner in which ADHD has come to be accepted as a regime of truth and invite others to be more critical of ideas presented as truth by social institutions.

The Meaning and Purpose of Autoethnography

To explain the meaning and purpose of autoethnography, I again draw heavily on Ellis and Bochner (2000: 739), who define autoethnography as

> an autobiographical genre of writing and research that displays multiple layers of consciousness connecting the personal to the cultural. Back and forth autoethnographers gaze, first through an ethnographic wide-angle lens, focusing outward on social and cultural aspects of their personal experience; then, they look inward exposing a vulnerable self.

As I describe my childhood, my school experience, my lack of career choice, I am giving the reader a glimpse into a way of life that once existed on Prince Edward Island. In so doing I am coming to realize how nature and nurture combined to mould me into the kind of person I became: obedient, shy and tractable, unwilling to step forward or speak out, actually never feeling I had the right to speak out, outwardly accepting the standards of the time and never questioning the imbalance of equality, but aware of it nevertheless, as I was aware of it during my experience of military life. I expect it is this sensitivity toward inequality that troubled me as I compared my son's school experience in the sixties with that of my grandson's in the nineties and that propelled me onto the path I am following. Along with documenting the changes in schools and schooling, I am providing a snapshot of the manner in which children's behaviour has lately been pathologized and sharing my grandson's experiences as one example of the negative impact of labelling.

But is my story truly an autoethnographic account? Again I draw on Ellis and Bochner (2000: 739–40), who confirm my opinion that I am engaging indeed in autoethnography:

> Like many terms used by social scientists, the meanings and appli-
> cations of autoethnography have evolved in a manner that makes
> precise definition and application difficult. It seems appropriate now
> to include under the broad rubric of autoethnography those studies
> that have been referred to by other similarly situated terms, such as
> personal narratives... narratives of the self... personal experience
> narratives... self-stories... first-person accounts... personal essays...
> ethnographic short stories... reflexive ethnographies..... Increasingly,
> however, autoethnography has become the term of choice in describ-
> ing studies and procedures that connect the personal to the cultural.

Ellis and Bochner suggest that "autoethnography provides an avenue for doing something meaningful for yourself and the world" (738). Through this process of writing and reflecting I have come to understand my strengths as well as my weaknesses and to make peace with the way I was. In writing Ben's story I am beginning to step away from that person to become a person who will speak out against perceived injustice, so that the lives of certain catego-rized children may become easier. In this way I give credence to Foucault's statement, quoted at the beginning of this chapter: "The main interest in life and work is to become someone else you were not in the beginning" (cited in Martin 1982: 10).

Ellis and Bochner (2000: 737) also point out that "by exploring a particu-lar life I hope to understand a way of life." By relating my story I am revealing a way of life which prevailed on rural Prince Edward Island during the last two-thirds of the twentieth century, before women had achieved the measure of equality they enjoy today. My story discloses the effects of the Depression, the influence of religion, the close connection between community and school and the way in which my limited choices had a direct impact on the direction of my life. As well, I am providing insight into the educational practices of the one-room schools, which had a far more inclusive approach than the schools of later periods, such as when my grandson attended. I am also documenting the changes that came about in school practices by that time and the effect those changes had on some children. In this way I have made clear two points made by Ellis and Bochner (2000): "The goal is to use your life experience to generalize to a larger group or culture" (737) and "In reflexive ethnographies, the researcher's personal experience becomes important primarily in how it illuminates the culture under study" (740).

Ellis and Bochner make one final point about the meaning and purpose of autoethnography: "The goal is to write meaningfully and evocatively about topics that matter and may make a difference" (742). This is what I have attempted to do, since the topic of labelling concerns me greatly and I feel that my story, if taken into consideration by educators, could have a positive impact on the education system. Yet, even as I see the value in disclosing my experience, I have not found it easy to make this very public journey down memory lane.

The Risks in Autoethnography

Clandinin and Connelly (2000: 62) alert us to the risk involved in "confronting our narrative past … because it makes secret stories public." As well, Ellis and Bochner (2000: 738) warn:

> The self-questioning autoethnography demands is extremely difficult … honest autoethnographic exploration generates a lot of fears and doubts — and emotional pain. … There's the vulnerability of revealing yourself, not being able to take back what you've written or having any control over how readers interpret it."

I have found that to be true, but because my account of Ben's painful journey may help other children, I am taking the risk. I concur with Clandinin and Connelly (2000) that "stories lived and told educate the self and others" (xxvi), which means that narrative "allows all of us to learn" (8). We can learn a great deal about our culture through Ben's story, a culture which promotes accountability and values conformity. Although my focus is on Ben, this is more than one child's story. It is representative of the stories of so many other children who spend their days trying to avoid hurt and humiliation as they navigate a school system that portrays them as failures because they learn differently. It has something to say about all children who are labelled.

It has something to say, certainly, about our culture, since, as Bruner reminds us, "human beings do not terminate at their own skins; they are expressions of a culture.... There is no such thing as human nature independent of culture" (cited in Bigge and Shermis 1999: 136). Our present culture appears to discourage independent thinking and to reward conformity in our children. And Michel Foucault would like us to be aware of the inherent danger in that.

Chapter Three

CRITICISM, CHALLENGE, CONFRONTATION AND CONFLICT

> It seems to me…, that the real political task in a society such as ours is to criticize the working of institutions which appear to be both neutral and independent; to criticize them in such a manner that the political violence which has always exercised itself obscurely through them will be unmasked, so that one can fight them. (Foucault, cited in Rabinow 1984: 6)

> Our own hearts, minds, spirits, and bodies, and those of our students, cry out that modern educational practices produce harmful and alienating effects that we should work together to undo. (Jardine 2005: 2)

Michel Foucault (1979, 1980, 1987), French philosopher, historian and scholar, viewed the world in a way that differs from the mainstream line of thought, and he encouraged us to do the same. I believe that the phrase "differs from the mainstream line of thought" is the key to understanding Foucault. The mainstream tends to accept established truth, traditions and institutions as permanent cornerstones of our society, values with which we should not tamper. But, if we allow ourselves to follow Michel Foucault's line of thought, we can see that the "taken-for-granted" should not be taken for granted, "that things weren't as necessary as all that" (Foucault, cited in Baynes, Bohman and McCarthy 1987: 104). We can see that the values we take for granted could easily have been different, had the power to establish them been vested in people with different views. We recognize that the beliefs and practices of social institutions such as schools have changed over the years and will change again, so we are within our rights to challenge the authenticity of any regime of truth promoted by any institution in our society. Following Foucault's line of thought we can begin to understand and to question how schools became invested with authority and power over the lives of children and families.

Of particular interest to Foucault are society's concepts of truth and knowledge and the way they are connected to power. He takes issue with the prevailing belief that scientific knowledge is the "real" truth, and he questions the notion of truth/knowledge as being fixed, universal or "disinterested," maintaining that society establishes its own "regimes of truth" (that is, bodies of knowledge which have been established as true) through discursive formations within disciplines such as psychiatry, psychology, medicine and education. These regimes of truth may change as society's standards and the discourses themselves change. Regimes of truth are interwoven with notions of power and subjectivity. In *Discipline and Punish* (1979) Foucault refers to western society as a disciplinary society, where humans are made both subjects and objects through a process he calls normalization, a society "which not only tells us what we must be and do, but how we must do it" (Jardine 2005: 49). Foucault would like us to be aware of the role of the human sciences in this process of subjectification ("the way in which a human being turns him- or herself into a subject" (cited in Rabinow 1984: 11) and objectification (which is done to the subject by others). Through his books, articles, lectures and interviews, Foucault invites us to take another look at the way human beings function in society and to question some of those tenets we have always assumed to be necessary, normal or indispensable. Jardine (2005: 9) reminds us:

> Foucault has given us many helpful insights and analytic tools to help us remember that those things which we most take for granted in our society and educational spaces as utterly obvious, necessary, natural, normal, or inevitable are not necessarily so, but are rather the result of human decisions that could have been made otherwise.

Therefore, we are within our rights when we question those decisions.

Foucault and Knowledge

Foucault challenges society's belief that the only knowledge acceptable as truth is that produced through scientific discourse. He argues that there are other equally valuable knowledges, which those in authority choose either to ignore or denigrate. Foucault refers to these forms of knowledge as "subjugated knowledges" (1980: 81). He contends that there are two sets of subjugated knowledges disqualified by society. On the one hand there are "historical knowledges," erudite knowledge affirmed by societies that have preceded us, beliefs associated with and accepted by past cultures which present society has discounted or somehow changed into some other form, "historical contents that have been buried and disguised" (1980: 81).[1]

> Those blocs of historical knowledge which were present but disguised within the body of functionalist and systematizing theory and which criticism--which obviously draws upon scholarship--has been able to reveal. (1980: 82)

On the other hand there are "local, popular knowledges," often originating from those in society who are marginalized, and, consequently, this knowledge is dismissed since it is not based on scientific observation:

> A whole set of knowledges that have been disqualified as inadequate to their task or insufficiently elaborated: naïve knowledges, located low down on the hierarchy, beneath the required level of cognition or scientificity. (1980: 82)[2]

Foucault believes that "it is through the re-appearance of this knowledge, of these local popular knowledges, these disqualified knowledges, that criticism performs its work" (1980: 82).

Foucault and Truth

It is the reluctance of our society to recognize these disqualified knowledges as truth, along with the way it establishes its narrow version of truth, that poses a problem for Foucault. As Jardine explains, his aim is to identify "*the underlying procedures and conditions* that needed to be present to allow any specific fact to be accepted as true, certain, knowledge" (2005: 88, emphasis in original). Foucault states:

> My problem is to see how men govern (themselves and others) by the production of truth (I repeat once again that by production of truth I mean not the production of true utterances but the establishment of domains in which the practice of true and false can be made at once ordered and pertinent). (1987: 108)

In this statement he makes very clear that when he speaks of truth he does not mean "the ensemble of truths which are to be discovered and accepted" (1980: 132), but rather "the ensemble of rules according to which the true and the false are separated and specific effects of power attached to the true" (132).

The tendency to regard truth as a commodity to be supported or suppressed, and to be adjusted according to the present needs and desires of society, fuels Foucault's conviction that one should be wary of any idea presented as a fixed truth. He also challenges the notion of "disinterested truth," maintaining that knowledge (truth) did not "slowly detach itself from its empirical roots ... to become pure speculation subject only to the demands of reason" (cited in Rabinow 1987: 7). Instead, Foucault sees it as manufactured by society and tied in with power, therefore always interested in a specific purpose:

> Truth is a thing of this world; it is produced only by virtue of multiple

forms of constraint, and it induces regular effects of power. Each society has its regime of truth, its "general politics" of truth; that is, the types of discourse which it accepts and makes function as true. (1980: 131)

Foucault goes on to explain the way in which a regime of truth is established: "'Truth' is linked in a circular relation with systems of power which produce and sustain it, and to effects of power which it induces and which extend it. A 'regime of truth'" (1980: 133). He adds that truth "is produced and transmitted under the control, dominant if not exclusive, of a few great political and economic apparatuses (university, army, writing, media)" (1980: 131–2). He speaks of a "triangle: power, right, truth," explaining that he means "the rules of right that provide a formal delimitation of power... the effects of truth that this power produces and transmits, and which in their turn reproduce this power" (93). Scientific knowledge lies within the parameters of this triangle, but other forms of knowledge (subjugated knowledges) do not.

Foucault and Power

Above all, Foucault wants us to understand the way power operates in society; he sees power as completely intertwined with knowledge and subjectivity. "It produces reality; it produces domains of objects and rituals of truth. The individual and the knowledge that may be gained of him belong to this production" (1979: 194). For Foucault, power and knowledge are never separate. "Knowledge and power are integrated with one another, and there is no point in dreaming of a time when knowledge will cease to depend on power" (1980: 52). He maintains that "truth isn't outside power or lacking in power" (131), adding, "the exercise of power itself creates and causes to emerge new objects of knowledge and accumulates new bodies of information" (51).

Jardine offers a classic example of the way that power and knowledge operate in unison in schools:

> The desire to more carefully monitor and classify children's "developmental needs" gave rise to whole new "objects of knowledge" to be explored, new "bodies of information." What then occurs is that the newly discovered "facts" about children provide the rationale for more carefully monitoring their development, and the exercise of power over children's lives that gave rise to the "facts" that provide this rationale disappears from view. (2005: 26)

Ben's ordeal speaks to the authenticity of Jardine's statement. Each test administered to him by psychologists seemed to reveal more questions about his ability, which necessitated further testing, and the accumulated information resulted in conflicting opinions on what to do, culminating in more labels, from the original assessment of ADHD to non-verbal learning disability to oppositional defiance disorder. The more tests that were administered to him, the more differences of opinion that were voiced, the more powerless he remembers feeling. He described himself as being yanked about like a puppet on a string by the experts acting on the knowledge they had acquired about him, as they explored different ways of dealing with what they saw as his disability.

Jardine's observation reinforces the validity of Foucault's concern about society's reliance on scientific truth. Foucault asserts that this dependence has led to the proliferation of human sciences which contribute to reducing people to objects: "That moment when the sciences of man became possible is the moment when a new technology of power and a new political anatomy of the body were implemented" (1979: 193). He reminds us:

> There can be no possible exercise of power without a certain economy of discourses of truth, which operate through and on the basis of this association. We are subjected to the production of truth through power and we cannot exercise power except through the production of truth. (1980: 93)

As he explores the way power operates in society, Foucault suggests that power is not easily explained or identified but is recognized mainly through its effects (Dumm 1996: 71). Baker (2001: 597) suggests that Foucault finds it easier to explain what power *is not* than what it is: "For Foucault it is not an essence, not a substance, not a possessed quantity, not the inherent quality of a gene or a cell, and it is not that which is used to justify domination... but that which explains how it works." It is an enabler. "Power produces things as it works through and on the body.... Foucault emphasizes power not to the point where it becomes almost impossible to see but to the point where it becomes almost impossible not to see it everywhere" (598).

Foucault understands power in a broader and more constructive sense than the narrower perception of it as being mainly repressive. He asks: "If power were never anything but repressive, if it never did anything but say no, do you really think one would be brought to obey it?" (1980: 119). Foucault suggests that power can also be a positive force, and that is the reason people accept it:

> What makes power hold good, what makes it accepted is simply the fact that it doesn't only weigh on us as a force that says no but that it traverses and produces things. It induces pleasure, forms knowledge,

produces discourse. It needs to be considered as a productive network which runs through the whole social body, much more than as a negative instance whose function is repression. (1980: 119)

Foucault further states that power is not a phenomena that is fixed in one individual or issues from a single site but, rather, is something which circulates through society in a circulatory system much like blood courses through the human body, and all humanity is caught up in exercising it or receiving its effects:

Power must be analyzed as something which circulates or rather as something which only functions in the form of a chain. It is never localized here or there, never in anybody's hands. ... Power is employed and exercised through a net-like organization. And not only do individuals circulate between its threads; they are always in the position of simultaneously undergoing and exercising this power. (1980: 98)

No one escapes its web. Foucault likens power to a

machine in which everyone is caught, those who exercise power just as much as those over whom it is exercised. ... Power is no longer substantially identified with an individual who possesses or exercises it by right of birth; it becomes a machinery that no one owns. (1980: 156)

Foucault believes that one can never be outside of power. As Baker suggests, it "subtly *penetrates* our thoughts, it is *seminal* in the construction of subjectivity, it *takes space* in and around our body, it *stimulates* responses and it *seduces, induces, produces*" (2001: 599, emphasis in original). It is the way this indefinable, invisible, yet pervasive power permeates our society and combines with knowledge to control and shape human bodies which concerns Foucault. He speaks of this combination as *disciplinary power,* power exercised "*within* the social body, rather than *from above* it" (1980: 39, emphasis in original)) and explains that it is through the working of disciplinary power that "human beings are made subjects" in our culture (cited in Rabinow 1984: 7). By "made subject," he means the way in which our society, which he identifies as *a disciplinary society*, combines power and knowledge to control and shape human bodies. The function of disciplinary power is "the control and transformation of behaviour" (Foucault 1979: 125) in order to produce "docile and useful bodies to staff our offices and factories, schools and armies" (Baynes et al. 1987: 97).

Foucault and Practices of a Disciplinary Society

Foucault specifies three practices which this disciplinary society uses to objectify humans and make them into subjects. They are 1) dividing practices, 2) scientific classification practices and 3) practices of self-formation. The first two are techniques of domination mainly exercised by others on a passive subject, while the third concerns what one does to oneself. During his schooling, Ben experienced all three practices.

Dividing practices are actions which set up binary oppositions such as *we/they, responsible/irresponsible, normal/deviant,* which result in the privileging of some individuals or groups and the exclusion of some, casting the latter in the role of the *other.* Harwood (2006: 83) understands dividing practices as "an efficient means to facilitate actions on the actions of others because they function to identify and isolate the individual. ... The subject is either divided inside himself or divided from others," showing that "dividing practices can have interior and exterior effects." They are those actions by which "the subject is objectified by a process of division either within himself or from others" (Foucault, cited in Rabinow 1984: 8), and they are prevalent in the education system. From the very first years of his elementary education, Ben was cast in the role of the other by teachers who seemed ready to view him as a potential problem. It didn't take him long to internalize their attitude toward him. He began to feel like an outsider in the company of his classmates.

Ball (1990: 4) explains dividing practices further:

> The use of testing, examining, profiling, and streaming in education, the use of entry criteria for different types of schooling, and the formation of different types of intelligence, ability, and scholastic identity in the processes of schooling are all examples of such "dividing practices."

They set the student apart from the student body, in the position of the other. Labelling students ADHD is an obvious dividing practice, a categorization which gives the subject both a social and a personal identity: "Using these techniques and forms of organization, and the creation of separate and different curricula, pedagogies, forms of teacher-student relationships, identities and subjectivities are formed, learned and carried" (Ball 1990: 4). Closely connected to dividing practices is scientific classification.

Scientific classification practices, employed in what are known as the human sciences, is another way Foucault suggests that humans are turned into objectified subjects. He suggests that the sciences "employing the root 'psycho'" (1979: 193) in particular, individualize persons, making them into objects of study. Developmental and educational psychology, which enjoy widespread popularity in the present school system, appear to do just that. Baker (2001: 10) elaborates on the enormous influence that developmental psychology may exert on a child's school experience, life experience and, ultimately, sense of self:

> Developmental Psychology… has become well placed to help define who or what someone is, what they are capable of and what experience someone is allowed to have on that basis. It has become the expert discipline in institutionally asserting what Gilles Deleuze calls "ways of existing." This may appear innocuous and irrelevant if the ways of existing authorized through developmental psychology had not become evidence of how the possibilities for Being, for humanness, for normalcy, for being valued by a school, had been narrowed to only certain versions.

The knowledge gained on the child through tests and observation places the child in a certain category, labelling her or him as a certain kind of learner. As Ben's experience evidences, bearing the label ADHD, as a result of testing by psychologists and other experts, can have a devastating effect on a child, since it is not one of the "ways of being" valued by the school. It also tells what schools value: order, discipline, compliance. It can be one unhappy result of the weaving together of knowledge and power.

Peters and Burbules (2004: 44) explain: "For Foucault knowledge in the human sciences is not disinterested, neutral, objective, or value-free: rather it is inextricably entwined with relations of power." Through the human sciences, Foucault asserts, individuals have been targeted, their behaviour monitored, interpreted and assessed, which results in their being consigned to certain categories. Again, this was Ben's experience. Burman (1994) corroborates this statement of Foucault's, noting:

> Developmental psychology participated in social movements explicitly concerned with the comparison, regulation, and control of groups and societies, and is closely identified with the development of tools of mental measurement, classification of abilities and the establishment of norms. (cited in Baker 2001: 625–6)

Educational and developmental psychology are particularly influential disciplines in education circles and exert a great deal of power over the lives of children, many of whom are adversely impacted by these tools of measurement and classification.

The third way Foucault asserts that humans are objectified is a form of subjectification known as self-formation, and it deals with the "way a human turns him- or herself into a subject" (cited in Rabinow 1984: 11). Self-formation comes about through many different "operations on [people's] own bodies, on their own souls, on their own thoughts, on their own conduct" (11). It involves a process of self-understanding "mediated by an external authority figure" (11). For a child in the school system, the external authority figure is usually the teacher. According to his or her experiences at school, the child begins to see him or herself in a certain light, as clever and capable or stupid and useless, as worthy or worthless. These feelings may be based on teacher attitudes, achievement tests and teacher evaluation. Gradually, the child constructs an identity based on the results of these encounters and on perceptions about how others regard him or her. For a child labelled ADHD, the process of self-formation may result in feelings of alienation, isolation and worthlessness, which contribute to a negative sense of self. Ben's gradual loss of self-esteem, due in part to a great deal of negative criticism from authority figures, culminated in his depiction of himself as a "loser."

Self-formation is connected to dividing practices, since the sense of self may be influenced by those dividing practices, which in turn are connected to scientific classification. All three contribute to the "bodily docility" with which all teachers are familiar (Jardine 2005: 41). "Our knowledge of the child is an investiture of our power over their bodies, their motility, and their lives. And of course all of this is done for their own good" (43).

Foucault and the Technologies of Power

Foucault suggests that the success experienced by a disciplinary society in implementing these three practices and producing useful docile bodies stems from the use of three instruments of power. He calls them *surveillance, normalization* and *the examination,* the latter of which is a combination of the first two (1979: 170). Possibly nowhere in our society, except in prisons, are these instruments of power more prominent than in our schools.

Surveillance is a technique which society uses for maintaining control, sustaining the belief that control over people can be maintained by observing them. "It is the fact of being constantly seen, of being able always to be seen, that maintains the disciplined individual in his subjection" (Foucault 1979: 187). It is through constant monitoring and observation that knowledge is gained of individuals, and through which power is exercised by all institutions in society, including the schools. "A relation of surveillance, defined and regulated, is inscribed at the heart of the practice of teaching, not as an additional or adjacent part, but as a mechanism that is inherent to it and which increases its efficiency" (176). In school, children are perpetually supervised, always under the gaze of an authority figure. In class their work is assessed and documented. Records are kept of their progress. On the playground and on the school bus their actions are observed. They soon come to believe that that even when there is no visible supervisor, they are still being watched and judged and behave accordingly. They learn to self-monitor, to try to adapt their behaviour to the expectations of the teacher. They become normalized.

Normalization of each individual is the goal of a disciplinary society, whose forces include "the beliefs, expectations, values, and practices which not only dictate what we should say, do, feel, value, and think, but reward or punish us if we fail to comply with the standards built into them" (Jardine 2005: 25). Dumm (1996: 101–2) describes normalization this way: "It is one of society's most profound innovations. … Through normalization, a continuous power is exerted on the body." It exercises a constant pressure to conform to society's standards so that everyone behaves in the same way. Those who do not or cannot are punished or excluded in some sense. Ben's experience of being excluded from his peers because of his inability to conform comes to mind.

One of the most influential agents of normalization is the media, which constantly presents and promotes fashions, lifestyles and role models. Youth, in particular, are vulnerable to these normalizing influences. Normalization involves comparison, differentiation, hierarchization, homogenization and exclusion (Foucault 1979: 183). Individuals are compared, differences noted, ranked according to performance, encouraged to conform and, if they do not, are marginalized by society. "By normalization, Foucault means the establishment of measurements, hierarchy, and regulations around the idea of a distributionary statistical norm within a given population — the idea of judgement based on what is normal and thus what is abnormal" (Ball 1990: 2). Foucault lays it out in this manner:

> First the definition of behaviour and performance on the basis of the two opposed values of good and evil; instead of the simple division of the prohibition… we have a distribution between a positive pole and a negative pole; all behaviour falls between good and bad marks, good and bad points. (1979: 180)

Jardine makes the following observation:

> The ranking of individuals' performance with reference to a norm (from the most to the least successful, from good to bad, from highest to lowest achievement) by a person of superior knowledge and power is one of the major tools used by a disciplinary society. (2005: 68)

She notes that this custom may increase efficiency, but it also serves to marginalize and devalue those who do not conform to society's expectations. Schools are forceful advocates of normalizing techniques, and children are the innocent victims of this push to normalize. "The Normal is established as a principle of coercion in teaching with the introduction of a standardized education and the establishment of *ecoles normales* (teachers' training colleges)" (Foucault 1979: 184). Schools have a set curriculum, grades, standardized tests and examinations. Children are tested, assessed and classified. If they do not conform to "normal" standards (academic or social), they are labelled and often medicated to help them become normalized. If they fail to succumb to the forces of normalization, often through no fault of their own, they are punished or excluded. This is often the fate of children whose nonconforming actions have earned them the label ADHD. It certainly proved to be Ben's fate.

The examination, according to Foucault, is another technique of control, a combination of surveillance techniques and normalizing judgment:

> It is a normalizing gaze, a surveillance that makes it possible to qualify, to classify, and to punish.... At the heart of the procedures of discipline, it manifests the subjection of those who are perceived as objects and the objectivation of those who are subjected. (1979: 184–5)

According to Peters and Burbules (2004: 63), it is on the basis of this "normalizing gaze" that "individuals can be judged as acceptable or deviant." Through the examination, human beings are monitored, judged, assessed and compared with others. "It engages them in a whole mass of documents that capture and fix them" (Foucault 1979: 189). School examinations force individuals to study and to show what they know. The results are recorded. In this sense, "the examination combines the deployment of force and the establishment of truth.... It is at the center of the procedures that constitute the individual as effect and object of power, as effect and object of knowledge" (1979: 184, 192). Foucault takes up the notion of the individual as a case: "*The examination surrounded by all its documentary techniques, makes each individual a 'case':* a case which at one and the same time constitutes an object for a branch of knowledge and a hold for a branch of power" (191, emphasis in original). It is a true instrument of disciplinary power.

Through his analysis of the way power and knowledge combine in our disciplinary society to produce "regimes of truth," Foucault makes manifest the insidious ways that society exercises control not only over our bodies but also over our minds, and he wants us to be aware of this. He does not mean to alarm us. As we go about our daily routine, raising families, paying mortgages, contributing to our communities, he would like us take every opportunity to "throw off familiar ways of thought and look at the same things in a different way" (1987: xxi). That exercise could lead us "to critique modernist Western knowledge and practices and create new possibilities" (Jardine 2005: 5). Foucault asks no less of us than that. And one of the most useful tools he has provided us for the purpose of critiquing is genealogy.

Genealogy

Genealogy offers an explanation for how concepts have evolved. Foucault presents a detailed and challenging explanation in *Power/Knowledge* (1980: 83), describing genealogy as "a form of history which can account for the constitution of knowledges, discourses, domains of objects etc.... [and] the union of erudite knowledge and local memories which allows us to establish a historical knowledge of struggles and to make use of this knowledge tactically today." What genealogy does, according to Foucault "is entertain the claims to attention of local, discontinuous, disqualified illegitimate knowledges against the claim of a unitary body of theory which would filter, hierarchise and order them in the name of some true knowledge" (83). In plainer language, genealogy traces the history of an idea or a practice from its first appearance down to the present, showing the disruptions, continuities and discontinuities, what knowledge was allowed and what was disallowed. This process illustrates how an idea or practice has evolved over time and has sometimes become something entirely different. In some cases, genealogy reveals that an idea or a practice which did not exist in the past has recently been accepted as reality, one of those "regimes of truth" which society promotes and, which Foucault asserts, "can be criticized and destroyed" (1982: 9).[3] In agreement with Foucault, other scholars offer similar thoughts on genealogy. It could be called a history of the present (Popkewitz and Fendler 1999: 185). "Genealogy is concerned with the processes, procedures, and apparatuses whereby truth and knowledge are produced" (Tamboukou and Ball 2003: 4). Genealogy "seeks to demonstrate the interweaving of what is said with what is done" (Baynes et al. 1987: 97).

One purpose of genealogy, then, is to question the notion of a fixed or universal truth, "to show that things weren't as necessary as all that ... rediscovering the connections, encounters, supports, blockages, plays of force, strategies, and so on that at a given moment establish what subsequently counts as being self-evident, universal and necessary" (Baynes et al. 1987: 104). Another useful purpose is "to discover the point at which a *particular* discourse emerged from these techniques and came to be seen as true" (Foucault, cited in Rabinow 1984: 7).

One of the "educational practices" which has evolved through discourse and may produce harmful and alienating effects on children is the label ADHD, and we need to question its truth. A genealogy of ADHD could demonstrate that this phenomenon is composed of discontinuous, disqualified, illegitimate knowledge, that it is not self-evident, and could show as well "its complex interconnection with a multiplicity of historical processes" (Foucault 1987: 103). It could show, therefore, that ADHD is not a fixed or universal truth but simply one of the regimes of truth which our society has accepted and made function as true.

Genealogy of ADHD

Attention deficit hyperactivity disorder, commonly known as ADHD, emerged in educational circles during the 1980s, and, among those who have researched this phenomenon, there are both skeptics and advocates of its validity. Conrad (1975, 1992), Conrad and Schneider (1980), Armstrong (1995) and Shrag and Divoky (1975) view it primarily as an approach to the control of the child, whereas Barkley (2002) is adamant that ADHD is a serious neurological disorder. According to Grantham (1999), the conceptual history of ADHD as a neurological disorder, which has undergone a number of twists and developments, can be traced back over one hundred and fifty years, when it was noted as a certain pattern of behaviour. In the early 1800s, a German family doctor wrote stories which featured a boy with behaviour problems whom he called "Fidgety Phil" (Grantham 1999: 3). Fidgety Phil was likely the forefather of today's child who bears the label ADHD. Rafalovich further researched ADHD's conceptual ancestry, gleaning his information on its origins and symptoms mainly from medical literature published between 1877 and 1929. He indicates that, from as early as the nineteenth century, there was "an increasing drive to medicalize unconventional childhood behavior" (2001: 94). Rafalovich discovered that, in 1877, William Ireland, an Edinburgh physician, published an article which would prove to be significant in the development of a theory about unconventional child behaviour. Ireland's article focused on two medical concepts of that time, *idiocy* and *imbecility*. Ireland defined idiocy as extreme stupidity and imbecility as a much less severe mental deficiency, but he did not expand on how a distinction could be made between the two (Rafalovich 2001: 99–100). Then, in 1890, a British physician, Charles Mercier, endeavoured to explain the difference between idiocy and imbecility during his discussion of children with mental deficiencies. He described the idiot as one who functioned at such a low level that he could not even adapt to his physical surroundings, whereas the imbecile was much less impaired. The imbecile could manage his physical environment but could not be educated to make a living. Mercier determined imbecility to be "a failure to meet the demands of social and institutional expectations" (Rafalovich 2001: 101). Mercier then linked behaviours exhibited by the imbecile to a person's inability to display "moral restraint and lawful behaviour," naming these traits "moral imbecility" (101). Physicians of that period understood the attainment of morality to be "a problem of human biological development" (101); moral behaviour had become a medical problem. In an article written in 1900, Ireland argues: "The title 'moral imbecility' is so far correct that there are certain children who show from the beginning a proneness to evil, a callous selfishness, and a want of sympathy with other people which is the most striking part of this disorder" (cited in Rafolavich: 102). Children with antisocial behaviours from then on were deemed to exhibit moral imbecility, a flawed condition in which other human faculties such as intelligence were considered normal or even above normal. This genealogical analysis by Rafalovich shows clearly how the language related to the behaviour of children has changed dramatically over time.

In 1902, an English pediatrician, George Still, questioned whether the lack of moral control in these *other children* (as opposed to *normal children*) might have a neurological basis. According to Rafalovich, "Still provided the groundwork for a category of mental illness that is, in practicality, specific to child deviance" (107). Dr. Still felt that the children, in spite of displaying antisocial behaviour, were neither criminal nor stupid and suspected that the cause of the behaviour was hidden inside the brain. He argued that "moral control can only exist where there is a cognitive relation to the environment" (cited in Rafalovich: 104), and he conjectured that the problem might be some sort of brain trauma, urging extensive examination and more methodical child study. Rafalovich connects Still's plea for scientific study to the process of objectification discussed by Foucault in *Discipline and Punish* (1979). Rafalovich also proposes that "Still's work is significant for the examination of the early discourse surrounding ADHD, and represents a break from the more general discussions of morality" (107).

The next development in analysis of this unconventional behaviour occurred during the 1920s when an outbreak of encephalitis occurred in England, and it was observed that children who recovered from this disease were often unruly and antisocial. Their symptoms, which included emotional instability, hyperactivity, poor motor control and oppositional behaviour, were believed to be the result of brain damage caused by the encephalitis. "The postencephalitic child was not responsible for his or her actions" (Rafalovich: 109). Many of the children were institutionalized. The diagnosis *encephalitis lethargica* now replaced the term "moral imbecility" because it provided an organic cause for many of the same symptoms.

In 1937, researcher Charles Bradley discovered that the amphetamine Benzedrine (closely related to the stimulant Dexedrine), which relieved headaches in encephalitis patients, also improved the conduct of difficult children. It was unusual in that it subdued rather than stimulated these children. This was the beginning of medicating children to control unmanageable behaviours. However, the use of stimulants to control childhood behaviours was not given extensive coverage in medical literature during the next few years. In 1947, researchers Strauss and Lehtinen conceived the label "minimal brain damage" to identify children suffering from *encephalitis lethargica* along with those who were displaying hyperactive behaviour but had never had encephalitis. These latter children were thought to have suffered brain damage at birth. In the United States, researchers tried to establish a link between behaviour problems in school and brain dysfunction since most of the children with problem behaviour had never had encephalitis. In 1957, according to Conrad and Schneider (1980), researchers Laufer, Denhoff and Solomons introduced the label "hyperkinetic impulse disorder" to describe unusual behaviour patterns (hyperactivity, impulsivity, inattentiveness) similar to those with organic causes but, in the case of some children, with no evidence of being related to a body organ. Hyperkinesis became the new category. Conrad, who suggests that all deviant behaviour is a social construction, attributes the diagnosis of hyperkinesis to a combination of clinical and social factors. The clinical factors include Bradley's discovery that amphetamines improved the conduct of unruly children and the development of the drug Ritalin by the pharmaceutical company CibaGeneva during the mid-fifties. In 1961 the U.S. Food and Drug Administration (FDA) approved the use of Ritalin for children diagnosed with hyperkinesis. The social factors consisted of the growing interest in children's mental health, increased government action and the pharmaceutical revolution. Other psychoactive drugs (those which effect the central nervous system), Benzedrine and Dexedrine, were also approved and promoted after the 1960s.

In 1966 a task force backed by U.S. Public Health Service and the National Association for Crippled Children and Adults worked to bring about an understanding of the term used to describe children's behaviour disorders. Out of three dozen diagnostic labels, this task force chose "minimal brain dysfunction" to cover a wide range of disorders, including hyperkinesis. The emphasis shifted from brain damage to brain dysfunction, with focus placed on inattentiveness and impulsivity. The labels "hyperkinetic syndrome" and "hyperactive child syndrome" were adopted and the use of Ritalin to control this behaviour was actively promoted during the late 1970s. According to Grantham (1999: 4), "there was a dramatic increase in studies on the use of amphetamines with children exhibiting hyperactive and impulsive behaviors."

In 1980, the *Diagnostic and Statistical Manual of Mental Disorders* (DSM-III), which is the main diagnostic reference of the American health profession, changed the name of this phenomenon from "hyperkinetic disorder" to "attention deficit disorder," with and without hyperactivity (Grantham 1999: 5). It listed the essential features as inattentiveness, impulsivity and hyperactivity, with a number of symptoms for each feature. In order to be diagnosed with ADHD, a child had to display at least three out of five symptoms for inattentiveness or impulsivity or two of five symptoms of hyperactivity. The onset of these symptoms must have been before the age of seven and must have been present for at least six months. The DSM-III estimated that 3 percent of American children suffered from this disorder and that it was ten times more common in boys than in girls. In 1987, the DSM-III-R included the label "attention deficit hyperactivity disorder" to show that the hyperactivity was as important as the inattentiveness (Woodrum 1994). In 1994, this manual was revised to DSM-IV and gave more detailed coverage of ADHD, addressing five areas. Inattentiveness, impulsivity and hyperactivity were still the essential features, but there were nine symptoms listed for each feature and the child had to display six out of the nine. DSM-IV suggested that 3 to 5 percent of children suffered from the disorder, with boys' diagnoses outnumbering girls' at a ratio of four to nine. DSM-IV admitted that no laboratory tests had been established to confirm the assessment of ADHD. In 2000, the DSM-IV-TR devoted over eight pages to ADHD, and it continues to maintain: "The essential feature of Attention-Deficit/Hyperactivity Disorder is a persistent pattern of inattention and/or hyperactivity-impulsivity that is more frequent and severe than is typically observed in individuals at a comparable level of development" (2000: 78). The manual also states that ADHD is prevalent in 3 to 7 percent of school-age children and acknowledges that there are still no laboratory tests or neurological assessments developed to diagnose this disorder. The DSM-IV-TR is now in the process of being revised to DSM-5, in which case ADHD may include more diagnostic criteria or may even be presented differently. Even though the DSM is considered to be the bible of the American Psychiatric Association, there have been questions raised about its scientific basis. *The Selling of DSM: The Rhetoric of Science in Psychiatry* (1992) challenges its diagnostic reliability, not least because the language of diagnoses evolves and changes to such an extent over time.

Since 1990, researchers who believe in the medical model keep hunting for evidence that ADHD is neurologically based. Russell Barkley, a fervent champion of the neurological model, continues to accentuate brain injury or abnormal brain development as the cause, even though the DSM-IV in 1994 acknowledged that no definitive tests have been authorized for diagnosing ADHD. In 1995, Barkley proposed a new label, "developmental disorder of self control" (Grantham 1999). No doubt this century will provide new names, new symptoms and new regimes of truth concerning this phenomenon, further extending its genealogy. However, the extreme changes in thinking demonstrated in this genealogy, ranging from mental deficiency to moral deviancy, to brain damage, to brain dysfunction, should disqualify any claims to a unitary theory or a "fixed truth" by the proponents of the diagnosis of ADHD.

A genealogy of ADHD certainly makes clear that the only knowledge accepted as true concerning this particular phenomenon is that provided by the medical profession, illustrating the observation made by Jardine (2005: 115) concerning Foucault's belief that "the rise of certain concepts, values, or practices (elements of knowledge) extends power to certain groups and not others." The following chapter, which presents a detailed genealogy of western society, provided by Foucault, explains how this appropriation of power by "certain groups" has come about.

Notes

1. In tracing the history of punishment, Foucault discovered that the practice of imprisonment implemented in the nineteenth century and practised ever since as the main form of punishment was not at all what the eighteenth-century reformers had in mind.
2. This might include an individual teacher's knowledge of a child's ability, which testing may not have revealed and which may even contradict the knowledge of the child accumulated through psychological tests, which is why it is usually considered irrelevant.
3. ADHD could be considered one such idea since it came into existence rather suddenly during the eighties.

Chapter Four

GOVERNMENTALITY, SCHOOLING AND SUBJECTIVITY

> I intend this concept of "governmentality" to cover the whole range of practices that constitute, define organize, and instrumentalize the strategies that individuals in their freedom can use in dealing with each other. Those who try to control, determine, and limit the freedom of others are themselves free individuals who have at their disposal certain instruments they can use to govern others. (Foucault 1997: 300)

How did it happen that our social system has evolved in such a way that almost every aspect of our lives is controlled? How did it come about that we, supposedly free individuals living in a democratic society, are so surrounded by rules and regulations, some self-imposed, that severely restrict our freedom? How did schools become sites for the control and colonization of children? How did the medical profession get control of our physical and mental health, with the authority to decide what constitutes illness? Michel Foucault, in his analysis of modern western society, provides the key to the enigma of social control by leading us to understand "the present through the past" (Walshaw 2007: 13).

Foucault's Genealogy of Modern Western Society

In *Discipline and Punish* (1979), Foucault presents a genealogy of modern western society from the classical age (which extends from the middle of the seventeenth century to the French Revolution) up to the latter half of the twentieth century. He documents the gradual formation and transformation of our society through stages (sovereign state, disciplinary society, governmentality approach) in order that we might understand the way the power of the state over the individual has developed. It may also help us to understand how the school has developed such power over the lives of children. Foucault says: "My objective, instead, has been to create a history of the different modes by which, in our culture, human beings are made subjects" (cited in Rabinow 1984: 7).

Discipline and Punish deals specifically with the creation of our modern penal system, but Foucault makes clear on the last page that the book applies to many other aspect of society: "At this point I end a book that must serve as a historical background to various studies of the power of normalization and the formation of knowledge in modern society" (308). He also asserts:

> This book is intended as a correlative history of the modern soul and of a new power to judge; a genealogy of the present scientifico-legal complex from which the power to punish derives its bases, justifications and rules, from which it extends its effects and by which it masks its exorbitant singularity. (23)

In the introduction to *The Foucault Reader*, Paul Rabinow paraphrases Foucault's words as he lays out the way our present social system evolved from one in which the king was concerned only in acquiring territory and had absolute power, towards one focused more on managing the population.

> The first major shift, therefore, is from a concern with the nature of the state, and then the prince and his concerns per se, to a broader and more detailed consideration of how to introduce economy and order from the top of the state down to all aspects of social life. Society was becoming a political target. (1984: 15)

With the shift from sovereign power, a new kind of power takes hold, which Foucault calls "bio-power," in which the state focuses on the human species (population, fertility) and the human body (as an object to be manipulated and controlled). Foucault reminds us that "the classical age discovered the body as the target and object of power" (1979: 136), and asserts: "The body becomes a useful force only if it is both a productive body and a subjected body" (26). In order to be productive, the body must be made docile, and he explains that "a body is docile that may be subjected, used, transformed and improved" (136). People working with the incarcerated population discovered that practices such as constant supervision and meticulous recordkeeping were useful in controlling the prisoner and transforming the behaviour, as well as in compiling knowledge of that individual. "The prison became a sort of permanent observatory that made it possible to distribute the varieties of vice or weakness" (126). Soon the same techniques of surveillance and documentation were adopted by other institutions, such as schools and hospitals, leading to Foucault's observation: "Is it surprising that prisons resemble factories, schools, barracks, hospitals, which all resemble prisons?" (228).

Society has by this time, according to its genealogical history as analyzed by Foucault, arrived at a stage which focuses on controlling the human body. Foucault elaborates on this disciplinary society, which "not only tells us what we are to be and do but how we must do it" (Jardine 2005: 49). Foucault proposes that in today's society people feel they are always being seen and judged so they have developed self- monitoring strategies. He labels the western world "a Panoptican society," referring to the Panoptican, a type of circular prison envisioned by Jeremy Bentham, whereby prisoners could be observed constantly but were unable to see the person watching them. Since they never knew when they were being observed, they modified their behaviour on their own. Thus, power was exercised in an invisible way through normalizing strategies and techniques, such as surveillance, that were internalized by people and acted as a form of social control. During the nineteenth century, with the birth of the human sciences, normalizing strategies expanded to include standards of normal and abnormal, which led to more individualizing techniques and more forms of subjectification (Foucault 1979).

Miller and Rose (2008: 5) advance the idea that *Discipline and Punish* presented new and different ways of thinking about power:

> The analysis of the birth of the prison extended Foucault's prior analysis of the administration of the self, and showed vividly how individualization was a way of exercising power. Despite its focus on the prison, discipline was no longer to be viewed as only carceral. Or, to put it differently, the engineering of conduct and the normalizing of behaviour that emerged within a carceral institution such as the prison provided a more generalized technology of social power. Such a perspective demonstrated the important normalizing role played by a vast array of petty managers of social and subjective existence, whether this occurred in the factory or the schoolroom.

Gradually, Foucault's understanding of power in our society expanded to include a more active role for the individual, whom he now saw possessed a certain degree of autonomy. He visualized power as working both outside and within the individual. True, the self was still subjected to power relations from institutions and other external systems, but it also possessed the power to resist those forces of domination and was actively involved in the process of self-formation. This was his theory of governmentality, which Margaret Walshaw perceives to be double-edged because "it both targets the individual as the means with which to maintain social control, and, at the same time, it provides the individual with the very techniques with which to resist this government of individualisation" (2007: 24). No wonder it is a difficult concept for the ordinary person to grasp.

The Concept of Governmentality

In analyzing how our western society so effectively manages its members, Foucault only rarely employs the words "social control." In *The History of Sexuality: Volume 1*, he does make use of the term, speaking of "agencies of social control" (1990: 119) and referring to the deployment of sexuality by the ruling class as "a defense, a protection, a strengthening, and an exaltation that were eventually extended to others, at a cost of different transformations, as a means of social control and political subjugation" (123). However, Foucault's work is saturated with similar terminology. He elaborates further on this concept of "governmentality" in *Ethics: Subjectivity and Truth*. He speaks of it as implying the relationship of the self to itself, providing an even more detailed definition, declaring:

> I intend this concept of "governmentality" to cover the whole range of practices that constitute, define, organize, and instrumentalize the strategies that individuals in their freedom can use in dealing with each other. Those who try to control, determine, and limit the freedom of others are themselves free individuals who have at their disposal certain instruments they can use to govern others. (1997: 300)

Foucault also refers to governmentality as an "ensemble formed by the institutions, procedures, analyses and reflections, the calculations and tactics, that allow the exercise of this very specific albeit complex form of power" (cited in Miller and Rose 2008: 27). And he suggests: "One could take up the question of governmentality from a different angle: the government of the self by oneself in its articulation with relations with others (such as one finds in pedagogy behaviour counseling, spiritual direction, the prescription of models for living and so on)" (Foucault 1997: 88).

Miller and Rose (2008) explain that "the term 'governmentality' sought to draw attention to a certain way of thinking and acting embodied in all those attempts to know and govern the wealth, health and happiness of populations" (2008: 54).

In the introduction to *Governmentality Studies in Education*, M.A. Peters (2009: xxxvi) draws on the work of Larner and Walters (2004), stating that this term has been used in the following two ways:

> (1) "a form of power whose logic is not the defense of territory or the aggrandizement of the sovereign but the optimization of the health and welfare of the population" and (2) "an approach that explores how

governing always involves particular representations, knowledges, and expertise regarding that which is to be governed."

Expertise in the psychological area is defined by Rose (1998: 11) as "the capacity of psychology to provide a corps of trained and credentialed persons claiming special competence in the administration of persons and interpersonal relations." He adds: "Psychology has produced a range of *new social authorities* whose field of operation is the conduct of conduct, the management of subjectivity" (63, emphasis in the original). And these new authorities, clinical, educational, and industrial psychologists, psychotherapists and counsellors, are highly regarded because of their skill. Rose concludes that a "significant theme" of the twentieth century and beyond is "the allocation of authority over the 'conduct of conduct' to experts" (156). He argues: "Convinced that we should construe our lives in psychological terms of adjustment, fulfillment, good relationships, self-actualization, and so forth, we have tied ourselves 'voluntarily' to the knowledges that experts profess (77).

Members of the medical profession consider themselves to be the experts in all areas relating to health and illness and seem to have the power and prestige to designate any type of behaviour as illness. P. Conrad, American medical sociologist (1975, 1992), has written extensively on the topic of medicalization as a form of social control. He has expressed concern over the way in which "certain forms of behavior in children have become defined as a medical problem and how medicine has become a major agent for their social control since the discovery of hyperkinesis" (1975: 12).

Other modern day scholars such as Majia Nadesan, Bernadette Baker, Margaret Walshaw and Thomas Popkewitz have researched Foucault's theory of governmentality as practised by our schools and the impact it has on the well being of our children. Surely schools qualify as institutions which deploy strategies that are used to control and govern others? Nadesan (2010: 8) observes that as early as the nineteenth century children were becoming "central targets" of "normalizing forces."

The Development of a Psychology of Childhood

By the early part of the twentieth century, interest in the mental health of children was growing. New classes of child experts such as pediatricians, child psychologists and child psychiatrists were engaged in research concerning child development and developed the psychology of childhood. "Experts strove to establish the characteristics of 'normal' stages of children's intellectual and social development" (Nadesan 2010: 41–2). For some years previously, experts in the field had been studying the behaviour of children, but the results did not stand up to the rigour demanded of scientific study because the observation had not taken place in a controlled environment. Now the establishment of clinics and nursery schools made it possible for psychological experts to observe large groups of young children of the same age in a controlled environment, to collect data and to construct norms. Rose explains the idea of the norm:

> A developmental norm was a standard based upon the average abilities or performance of children of a certain age on a particular task or in a particular activity. It thus not only presented a picture of what was *normal* for children of such an age, but enabled the normality of any individual child to be assessed by comparison with this norm. (1998: 110)

Andrew Gesell, working at the Yale clinic, monitored and treated children who were having problems at school. He also studied normal development of infants and toddlers. He developed standardized developmental scales that could be used to evaluate and diagnose young children and to establish divisions between normal and abnormal. Gesell's work made childhood "visible, inscribable, and assessable" through the use of charts, scales and observation schedules (Rose 1998: 111). In 1920, Jean Piaget advanced his "ages and stages" theory, which promoted belief that there were definite ages at which children should attain certain steps in their development. He published *Judgment and Reasoning in the Child* (1924), which "articulated 'normal' stages of childhood cognition, thereby enabling the identification of 'abnormal' or delayed cognitive development" (Nadesan 2010: 43). In 1939, Leo Kanner published *Child Psychiatry*, the first textbook in English familiarizing pediatricians with children's personality problems (43). Other books followed which illustrated and suggested ways of diagnosing social pathology. "As the definition and scope of what constituted a 'health problem' expanded to include interpersonal hygiene and, eventually, mental hygiene, expert authorities turned to explore and manage the social-psychic environment of America's children" (43). Rose (1998) advises that psychological assessments could take the form of "intelligence tests, development scales, personality assessments, or vocational guidance interviews" (112). He makes the following observation:

> The technical device of the test, by means of which almost any psychological schema for differentiating individuals may be realized, in a stable and predictable form, in a brief period of time, in a manageable space, and at the will of the expert, is a central procedure in the practices of objectification and subjectification that are so characteristic of our modernity. (112)

Schooling and Subjectification

Schools became the primary site for observing children. There, behaviour was scrutinized diligently in order to detect deviance so that early intervention could take place. It appeared that the more children were subjected to surveillance the more forms of problematic behaviour were detected. Nadesan (2010: 44) comments: "As a widening range of psychological neuroses and personality disorders were articulated in psychiatric vocabularies, educational psychologists, school health officials and parents were instructed how to identify incipient disorders and dangerousness in their otherwise 'normal' children."

The profusion of information, expertise and ongoing research on the subject of childhood by psychological experts, which has been available and widely disseminated since the early twentieth century, provides the background and sets the stage for the widespread practice of testing and labelling, two of the strategies used in the governance of children so prevalent in our schools today. A result of testing is that children are sorted into categories and ascribed labels, including ADHD. In the school, the teacher acts as the agent of the state in many ways. She follows a curriculum, is required to meet outcomes and must discipline her class so that she provides an atmosphere that enhances their learning. She answers to the administration and must facilitate the internalization of societal values if she is to be considered a "good teacher." It is a teacher's job to ensure the students become models of the "good pupil." A red flag goes up immediately when children like Ben appear in the classroom, children who speak without putting up their hand, who forget and run in the corridors, who colour outside the lines and even colour carrots black. Such a student is not fitting in, and this behaviour is deemed to be in need of correction. This can lead to a process of assessment, whereby consultants, psychologists and psychiatrists are brought in to administer tests to determine and diagnose problems that are causing the behaviour. Efforts to establish normalized behaviour take place through medication, behaviour modification or educational programming. The assessment process often leads to the labelling of children, and parents, for the most part, may not be closely involved or may feel powerless to express their concerns because of the level of expertise that accompanies a diagnosis. This whole practice may be done with the best of intentions, but as Gail Jardine points out, "stated intentions and *actual* effects often differ, and when they do it is the actual effects that matter in people's lives" (2005: 31, emphasis in original).

Ben's experience in the school reveals how costly resistance can be for the student and for parents. Neither he nor his parents ever anticipated that, from the moment he entered the classroom, he would have to adapt to the school's standards and expectations with respect to the behaviour of a six-year-old student. When, in grade one, he did not conform to all the requirements of the teacher (staying at his desk for long periods, colouring pictures, listening intently even when he was not interested), he was targeted as a problem, referred for diagnosis to a psychologist and branded with a label that would haunt him throughout his years in the education system. Foucault's conception of "dividing practices" (1979) was brought to bear to set Ben apart from the six-year-olds who managed to internalize the codes of behaviour required by the school.

I compare Ben's experience with that of my six-year-old acquaintance James, who has recently entered the school system. I have known James since he was born. He is a friendly, outgoing little boy who loves people. He even skips up the aisle in church. Whenever I meet James, whether it is in church, at the library, on the road, at a shopping mall, with a group or alone, he waves and calls out loudly, "Hi Marion." That is, he greeted me enthusiastically until very recently. James started grade one last September. Three months later, I met him with a group of children. He looked at me, looked at the other children to see how they were reacting to my presence and then smiled rather tentatively without speaking. I meet him often since then, and I see how he has changed. At church, he walks sedately up the aisle. He never shouts a happy greeting to me or to anyone. He is still pleasant and polite but subdued and very aware of how a person in first grade is supposed to behave. His exuberance has been dimmed. And I am not the only one who has noticed the change in James. However, he is considered to be one of the best students in his grade one class, quiet, attentive and docile. And he loves school. It appears that the years of schooling will prove to be a more enjoyable experience for James than they were for Ben, who could not manage to conform. Yet I am saddened by the disappearance of James's spontaneity, and I wonder to myself: Is that what schools are supposed to be doing to our children? Is that an example of the colonization of childhood (Cohen 2006: 29)? What has James lost in this normalization process? It is difficult to reconcile the subjectification of our children in the school system with the notion that we live in a free society, a society "that proclaimed the limits of the state and respect for the privacy of the individual?" (Miller and Rose 2008: 1). Both children's stories speak to the effects of social control in the education system.

Conrad (1975, 1992) has researched and published extensively on hyperkinesis, on the medicalization of deviance and on the subject of medicalization as a form of social control. One of his concerns is that the drug treatment was available twenty years before the medical label was devised. In his journal article "The Discovery of Hyperkinesis: Notes on the Medicalization of Deviant Behavior" (1975), Conrad expresses unease over the way "certain forms of behavior in children have become defined as a medical problem and how medicine has become a major agent for their social control since the discovery of hyperkinesis" (12). Conrad and Schneider (1980) discuss at length the consequences of medicalizing issues such as childhood deviance, calling medical treatment "a new form of punishment and social control" (1). He expresses concern that the treatment is under the control of experts and that the individual, rather than society, is perceived to be the cause of the problem. He observes that it is much easier to blame the victim than it is to change the environment. And he argues that society could find this more costly in the long run.

Social Control

Social control, like Foucault's concept of power, is not easy to understand or define. Like power, it is "a pervasive factor of human social life" (Walshaw 2007: 20). Similar to Foucault's notion of power, social control can be recognized primarily through its effects as it spreads, web-like, through every level of society. If ordinary citizens think about it at all, social control probably appears to them to operate on individuals through a combination of the authority of government and the influence of their social milieu. They may not have grasped the notion that it emanates as well from somewhere within themselves. So it can be recognized as "power without a center, or rather with multiple centers" (Miller and Rose 2008: 9). We supposedly live in a democracy, but our freedom is at times severely curtailed. Certainly my story reflects a lack of freedom, due to the impact of the social code of the period, concerning women, childhood and masculine superiority, a code which I had, to a certain extent, internalized. Ben's freedom to realize his full potential was severely curtailed by a system of education which tried to impose on him a code of conduct he could not internalize.

Throughout many of his articles and lectures, Foucault challenges us to be aware of the subtle ways we are controlled and influenced by the medical profession and other societal institutions, such as schools, churches and universities, those institutions closest to the family. He urges us to be cognizant of these forces of social control which lead to degrees of subjectification that change our thinking and behaviour. Awareness sometimes can be difficult because we have been so indoctrinated into believing that the "way it is now" is the only way, that often we don't even realize how subtly we are being controlled by "institutions which appear to be both neutral and independent" (Foucault, cited in Rabinow 1984: 6). Anyway, questioning the system does not lead down an easy path. Ben and his parents discovered that. Perhaps it is time to respond to Foucault's challenge:

Maybe the target nowadays is not to discover who we are but refuse what we are. We have to imagine and to build up what we could be to get rid of [a] political "double bind" which is the simultaneous individualization and totalization of modern power structures. The conclusion would be that the political, ethical, social, philosophical problem of our days is not to try to liberate the individual from the state, and from the state's institutions, but to liberate us both from the state and from the type of individualization which is linked to the state. We have to promote new forms of subjectivity through refusal of this kind of individuality which has been imposed on us for several centuries. (cited in Rabinow 1984: 22)

Chapter Five

DISCOURSES AND THE
PURSUIT OF TRUTH IN ADHD

> My role ... is to show people that they are much freer than they feel,
> that people accept as truth, as evidence, some themes which have
> been built up at a certain moment during history, and that this so-
> called evidence can be criticized and destroyed. (Foucault 1982: 10)

Michel Foucault reminds us many times through his books and lectures that
society decides and promotes what it wants to be seen as true, and he explains
that society establishes its regimes of truth through *discourse*. He describes
discourses as "practices that systematically form the objects of which they
speak.... Discourses are not about objects; they do not identify objects, they
constitute them and in the practice of doing so conceal their own invention"
(cited in Ball 1990: 2). Discourses, then, are embedded in power relations. They
"are about what can be said and thought, but also about who can speak, when,
and with what authority. Discourses embody meaning and social relations,
they constitute both subjectivity and power relations.... Discourses constrain
the possibilities of thought. They order and combine words in particular ways
and exclude or displace other combinations" (2). The value people attach to
any discourse is influenced by the way power operates within and through
the language, as well as by who uses and circulates particular kinds of truths.

Foucault suggests that it is through the production of discourse that the
decision is made to subjugate some knowledges and dismiss them as unworthy
and to accept other knowledges as the truth. He refers to this whole process of
discussion, acceptance and rejection of ideas as "a production of true discourses
that serve to found, justify, and provide reasons and principles for these ways
of doing things" (1987: 108). It is through discourse that the guidelines for
"truth" are established.

ADHD is an example of a twentieth-century regime of truth that has been
constituted through education and medical discourse. It appears to have been
talked and written into existence by educators, psychiatrists, psychologists
and other professionals who have the power in their field, so they are the ones
who are heard. They have their own ideas of how children should behave, as
well as how they learn, and have managed to promote these ideas as "truths."

They have established the concept of *normal*, and as they studied children and grouped common characteristics together, developed a new *abnormal* category. This also has become a "truth." Since the eighties, some children who do not conform to certain accepted patterns of behaviour, who have difficulty sitting quietly and listening, who are motivated in a different way and who learn by doing, have been labelled as having attention deficit hyperactivity disorder. Through the years before that, the names and the meanings attached to active behaviours have changed many times through discourse, from ascribing them as mental illness or moral deviance to suggesting brain damage or brain dysfunction. And the arguments persist over ADHD, concerning its validity, its origin and its treatment. Discussions continue over whether it is caused by neurological, biological or environmental factors, or whether the range of behaviours described as part of ADHD are, in fact, perfectly normal.

It is through discourse that ADHD has been medicalized. The voices which have been heard the loudest are those that insist that ADHD is a disorder with a neurological basis. The American Psychiatric Association's publication *Diagnostic and Statistical Manual of Psychiatric Disorders* (2000) has enormous influence in the United States and many other parts of the world, including Canada. It lists ADHD as a neuro-biological disorder with the most common treatment being amphetamines. This has contributed to the medicalization of ADHD. The "expert" has credentials and is authorized by society to categorize children. The "doctor" is trusted to use her knowledge for the good of society. The powerful pharmaceutical companies continue to promote the use of drugs as a form of treatment and profit from the results. Yet other researchers articulate their belief that ADHD is caused by societal factors. They do not have as much power or the medical credentials, so their "truth" is not fully accepted. Many others, including parents, teachers and researchers, assert that ADHD is not a disorder, that it is simply another learning style. In most cases, their voices are not heard. These are more examples of subjugated knowledges, and they are all part of the discourse surrounding ADHD.

Although the American Psychiatric Association defines ADHD as a neuro-biological disorder, not all researchers and scholars concur with that definition and through study and research have arrived at their own interpretations. Some scholarly articles refer to ADHD as a social construction (Conrad and Schneider 1980; Conrad 1992), an enterprise (Cohen 2006), a disability (Smith, Polloway, Patton and Dowdy 1998), a fad (Kohn 1998), a dysfunction (Schwean, Parkinson, Francis and Lee 1993), a cultural phenomenon (Armstrong 2006) and a bio-medical construct (Cooper 2001). McCluskey and McCluskey (2003: 32) contend that ADHD is "perhaps the most widely discussed, referred, diagnosed and misdiagnosed condition in North America."

It is little wonder that parents have difficulty sifting through the flood of information, often conflicting, on this controversial issue. The information focuses on four main themes: the validity of ADHD as a physical or medical condition, the medicalization of ADHD, diagnosing ADHD, and inclusion and exclusion practices in schools.

Validity of the ADHD Label

If we examine the ADHD label through a Foucauldian lens, we can find reasons to question its validity. Foucault (1977) persuasively articulates his belief that truth is not a concept just lying around waiting to be discovered but is *"created/ constituted* to serve the interests and circumstances of the human beings in each era" (cited in Jardine 2005: 81, emphasis added). He calls these concepts, created through discourse, "regimes of truth," and he argues that the validity of any regime of truth can be challenged. As mentioned, he says that his role, the role of the intellectual

> is to show people that they are much freer than they feel; that people accept as truth, as evidence, some themes which have been built up at a certain moment during history, and that this so called evidence can be criticized and destroyed. (1982: 10)

According to Foucault, all types of classification are truths manufactured by society and, therefore, can be criticized and destroyed. As previously stated, he calls them dividing practices and indicates that it is through the human sciences, particularly educational and developmental psychology, that school children are classified as certain kinds of learners. In a classroom, children labelled ADHD become the *other*, since it is "a way of existing" not valued by the school. It sets children apart from other students, marking them as different and somehow less worthy than their so-called "normal" classmates. The establishment of ADHD is one of the more recent regimes of truth in today's society since it only appeared on the education stage in 1980. Foucault urges people to speak out against all such dividing practices, all such regimes of truth, and to refuse to accept them as true.

Barkley is one scholar who is passionate in his belief that ADHD exists and has expressed his certainty in many articles. He is responsible for the publication of "International Consensus Statement on ADHD," authorized by "a consortium of international scientists" (2002: 89), which specifies that all of the major medical associations and government health organizations in the United States recognize ADHD as a genuine disorder. In a two-page document, signed by over eighty scientists, he details the reasons that scientists have confirmed its status as a neurological, psychological disorder. The document also expresses his grave concern over the "inaccurate" portrayal of ADHD by the media, which has provided coverage of views both opposing and supporting this scientific belief, "as if both sides had equal merit" (89). Through the skilful use of language, Barkley strives to make the reader believe that his views are the real and only "truth" about ADHD. He lists the prestigious medical organizations which share his view of ADHD. He alludes to his colleagues as "international scientists" and repeatedly uses the word "disorder" when referring to ADHD. At the same time, he attempts to make those who have said that ADHD is not a disorder appear less credible by speaking disparagingly of opposing theories as "the views of a handful of nonexpert doctors" (89) and "fringe doctors whose political agenda would have you believe there is no real disorder here" (90). In a final burst of rhetoric, he asserts that to depict ADHD as not being a real disorder is as misleading as declaring that the earth is flat (2002: 90). Maclure (2003: 80) reminds us that even scientific discourse is not devoid of rhetoric:

> Like any other texts, research texts … are "fabrications." Their truths and findings are put together — that is built or woven (depending on the sense of "fabric" that one prefers) to achieve particular effects and structures — rather than artlessly culled from a pre-existing world Out There. As we have seen, this is never an innocent business.

Maclure also informs us that there are ways of "troubling" the writing of any author. We can ask ourselves questions such as "Where does this text get its authority?" "How are knowledge claims established and defended?" "Whose voices are privileged in this text? Who is silenced?" (82). Such questions can help us to see beyond the rhetoric Barkley uses to establish his claim that ADHD is a valid condition.

In spite of Barkley's eloquent defence of the medical position and in response to Foucault's vision of the role of the intellectual, an increasing number of educators, scholars and other professionals have begun to question the legitimacy of the ADHD label. Contributors to *Critical New Perspectives on ADHD* (Lloyd et al. 2006) contest the theory that ADHD is a neurologically or biologically determined disorder. These academics identify ADHD as a phenomenon connected to society rather than to the child. Some of the factors to which they attribute the rapid rise of ADHD since 1980 include the following: the push for new markets by major pharmaceutical companies, the increasing dominance of U.S. psychiatric models, the changing approaches to schooling and the frantic pace of today's society, which leaves some parents unable to cope. They also have concern over the way the assessors arrive at the diagnosis.

Lloyd (2006) points out that the ADHD label is the result of a subjective assessment of a checklist of behaviours by professionals. She adds that these behaviours "have been clustered together *by human judgment* into a diagnosis" (215, emphasis added). She advocates doing away with labels, urging us to view children as individuals: "There are no ADHD students; there are individual children with very varied family and educational histories, competencies, learning styles and preferences" (223). She argues that "it does not make sense to sweep large numbers of children into one rather over-simple category, labeling and medicating them" (215). She believes that if schools encourage and help parents to become engaged, they will be less likely to look for labels in order to escape blame. But she also notes that the role of teachers has become more difficult due to new approaches to education which stress early attainment in basic skills and put more emphasis on tests and assessments. She also makes the very crucial point that the pharmaceutical companies are the driving force in the push to medicate children and are mainly responsible for the "mindset that views children in terms of normality and disorder" (220).

Tait (2006) questions the concept ADHD, seeing it as pathologizing normal behaviour and taking away moral responsibility from people, since the label often ensures that they are no longer held accountable for their actions. Like Baker, Tait blames the discipline of psychology for "*creating* difference" and "targeting human individuality" (pp. 93–4, emphasis in original). He believes that the scientific world has a long way to go before the truth of ADHD can be established since there is no agreement on any aspect of the disorder, its cause, its treatment, its prevalence or its long-term prognosis.

Cohen (2006) sees ADHD as an *enterprise* rather than a disorder. The label provides billions of dollars to schools to fund the special needs of children. It absolves parents of guilt over their childrearing methods, and "the label also provides schools yet another alibi to explain why they regularly fail to make some children fit in the only societal institution designed exclusively for children" (13). Instead of a genuine disorder, it is more like a list of behaviours that teachers find annoying. Cohen finds that "the diagnosis of ADHD and the drug Ritalin mark the beginning of the full scale psychiatric colonization of childhood" (29).

Armstrong maintains that the problem is with society, suggesting that children labelled ADHD "are the messengers of today's frenetic stressed-out culture" (2006: 34), and that "the so-called ADHD child's behaviors reveal much more about the context in which we live than about the specific mechanisms that reside within an individual brain" (34). He compares children labelled ADHD to "canaries in a coal mine" (34) and argues that these children should not be branded as defective but seen as a "kind of early warning signal for cultural instability" (34). Öngel (2006) agrees, characterizing the behaviours displayed by a child labelled ADHD "as the natural and understandable reaction of an insecure child to a stressful situation" (117). Jacobsen (2006) reasons that there is no conclusive way of deciding what is normal and what is abnormal because all children exhibit similar behaviours at one time or another. He suggests that labelling a child ADHD may just be a means of exerting power over children and wonders whether labelling could be considered a form of psychological abuse (171).

In their book, *The Myth of the Hyperactive Child*, researchers Schrag and Divoky express concern at the shift by American institutions toward medical treatment for children "who suffer from no scientifically demonstrable ailments but whose behavior is troublesome to adults" (1975: xi). They scoff at the notion of treating behaviour problems as illness and view it as a means of controlling the child. They warn that this process of screening, labelling and drugging children is "likely to have profound effects for the future," demonstrating to everyone that "if they don't conform, they too may be placed in one of those classes or be labeled as 'maladaptive'" (xvi). Schrag and Divoky point out that "an entire generation is slowly being conditioned to distrust its own instincts, to regard its deviation from the narrowing standards of approved norms as sickness and to rely on the institutions of the state and on technology to define and engineer its 'health'" (xvii).

Kohn (1998) and Specht (2002) are two more scholars who were ahead of their time in refusing to accept ADHD as a valid disorder. Kohn argues vehemently that we are labelling children unnecessarily. Instead of a disorder, he sees ADHD as a current fad around which an entire industry has grown, to the benefit of the pharmaceutical companies who manufacture the drugs administered to children labelled ADHD. Kohn believes that these children are simply restless because of rigid classroom structuring and proposes that a more appropriate title than ADHD might be NDEM — not docile enough for me (14). Kohn notes that researchers have observed that it is in classrooms where children are required to remain inactive for long periods of time that they become restless and inattentive, two of the behaviours attributed to ADHD. Kohn concludes that, if after a hundred years of discussion, there is still no consensus among professionals as to the origin, nature and treatment of ADHD, it's reasonable to question its authenticity. Specht too questions its validity, suggesting that "perhaps our current attitudes and understandings of learning exceptionalities will go the way of our beliefs about the left-handed child" (2002: 6), who was believed to be influenced by the devil and forced to conform to the right-handed norm. Seeing left-handedness as an abnormality was a "regime of truth" from a previous era which has now been invalidated, verifying Foucault's position that what people believe to be permanent truths often change over the course of history.

Medicalization of ADHD

Of all the controversies that have raged around ADHD, the issue that has ignited the most furious debate seems to be the contention by many in the medical profession, by some parents and by other professionals in the field that the phenomenon known as ADHD is a neuro-biological disorder requiring medical treatment, in other words, medicalization.

The *Diagnostic and Statistical Manual of Mental Disorders* (2004), as previously mentioned, defines it as a neuro-biological disorder and suggests that the preferred treatment is medication. In the United States and Canada, and therefore Prince Edward Island, ADHD is widely viewed as a medical problem, and Ritalin has traditionally been the drug of choice for treatment. The National Institute of Mental Health (NIMH) concurs with this definition and provides a detailed booklet on ADHD, which, among other things, offers advice on medical treatment in pre-schoolers, school-age children, teen-agers and adults, noting that "for decades, medications have been used to treat the symptoms of ADHD" (2004: 9). This booklet includes a list of stimulants, with the "approved age," meaning that "the drug has been tested and found safe and effective in children of that age" (9). Three of the stimulants, Adderall, Dexedrine and Dextrostat, according to this booklet, may be prescribed for children as young as three. Other stimulants listed are Concerta, Focalin, Metadate ER, Ritalin (extended release and long acting) and Cylert. This last drug is the only one about which the NIMH provides a warning about possible serious side effects. The NIMH, in this text, advises: "About 80 percent of children who need medication for ADHD still need it as teenagers. Over 50 percent need medication as adults" (11). This information, from such influential sources, so readily available on the Internet, carries a lot of weight with other countries.

Yet there are many in the medical and education fields, in the United States, the United Kingdom, Australia and Canada, as well as other countries, who argue persuasively that ADHD has a sociological rather than a biological basis. As mentioned previously, Conrad, a sociologist who has written extensively on the medicalization of many behaviours in western society, refers especially to the way that certain behaviours of children have been medicalized, particularly since the discovery of hyperkinesis during the fifties. He defines medicalization as a "process by which nonmedical problems become defined and treated as medical problems, usually in terms of illness or disorder" (1992: 209). In *Deviance and Medicalization: From Badness to Sickness* (1980), Conrad and Schneider argue that our society has seen a growing change in the way behaviour, including children's behaviour, is defined What was once considered disruptive, sinful or criminal is now viewed as illness; in other words, deviance has become medicalized. Conrad believes deviance to be a social construction: that there can be no society without rules and norms and that deviance simply signifies behaviour that does not conform to social norms. Conrad attributes the medicalization of so-called deviant behaviours to such social factors as the decreasing influence of religion, society's steadfast faith in science and the growth of prestige and power of the medical profession, which has authority over anything labelled sickness. He points out that the drug treatment for hyperactivity in children was available twenty years before the medical label was devised and offers an explanation why the childhood behaviour hyperkinesis, which had been virtually unknown up until 1960, became during the 1970s "the most common child psychiatric problem" (14). According to Conrad (1975), two factors contributing to the popularity of the diagnosis were the burgeoning pharmaceutical industry and government action. During the sixties the pharmaceutical companies actively promoted their drugs, especially targeting education and medical institutions. They advertised Ritalin and Dexedrine in medical journals, urging physicians "to diagnose and treat hyperkinetic children" (16). They disseminated information on this newly discovered disorder and its treatment through education circles, spending a quarter of their budget on promotion and advertising. At the same time, the U.S. government held hearings into the practice of prescribing drugs to treat hyperactive children. The hearings recommended that only physicians diagnose and prescribe treatment, that parents have a choice to accept treatment and that research continue on the long-term effects. Conrad and Schneider (1980) conclude: "This report served as blue-ribbon approval for treating hyperkinesis with phychoactive medications" (159).

Conrad is one of many who strongly believe that ADHD is a problem which originates in society rather than in the brain of a child, one of many who advocate that the use of drugs to control it is completely unwarranted. Many of these professionals are convinced that changes in the child's environment, particularly in the education system, will be far more beneficial to the child than a Ritalin prescription. However, in spite of the information available concerning the role society plays in the ADHD phenomenon, Lloyd (2006) observes: "There is also, in Britain, the USA, and other countries, clear evidence of a significant move towards greater use of psycho-medical explanations" (217). Norris and Lloyd (2000) report: "In England, between 1991 and 1996, the number of methylphenidate prescriptions increased by over two thousand per cent. The figures suggest that the number of prescriptions is on a strong

upward trend and that, as yet, there is little sign of the drug reaching satura-
tion point" (124).

Furthermore, research by Norris and Lloyd (2000) has determined that
a significant reason for the rise of ADHD as a medical problem, along with ag-
gressive marketing by pharmaceutical companies, availability of information
for parents on the Internet and changes in the education system, is the role of
the media in Britain, which had devoted a great deal of coverage to stories of
parents whose children were having difficulties in school. According to the
articles, these parents were convinced that their children were suffering from
a medical problem (ADHD), yet had struggled unsuccessfully to get a medical
diagnosis from their doctors, which would give the children access to the drug
Ritalin. So they took their battle to the media, publicly challenging the medical profession, accusing them of being uninformed about ADHD. *Informed* for
the parents "implied acceptance of the notion of ADHD and a willingness to
prescribe drug treatment" (Lloyd and Norris 1999: 506). Norris and Lloyd
(2000) argue that by printing almost exclusively the arguments of the parents,
the media oversimplify a complex problem and portray the parents as victims
of uninformed doctors, tipping the balance of public opinion in favour of
the parents and entrenching the belief that ADHD is a neurological disorder
controllable by drugs. Through all this coverage giving voice to parents, the
media were not only disseminating information but producing the discourses
around which ADHD is constructed. These discourses "continually define
normal behavior in apposition to the 'abnormal' behavior of children with
ADHD" (Norris and Lloyd 2000: 125), contributing to the production of "truth"
about ADHD. Norris and Lloyd conclude that the views of "many parents and
professionals are more influenced by what they read in the newspapers" than
by the "literally thousands of academic papers on ADHD" (136).

Lloyd (2006) points to other reasons why teachers and parents may promote the medicalization of ADHD. Teachers have discovered that it is easier
to procure funding from government for extra help in their classrooms when
students have been diagnosed as having a medical problem. As well, a medical diagnosis vindicates parents whose children have experienced difficulties
in school, and who have felt that teachers and society in general blame them
for their child's problems. Parents may prefer to have their child diagnosed
with a medical problem rather than with an emotional problem, believing
that there is less stigma attached to medical problems. For these parents, the
medical diagnosis provides "labels of forgiveness" (Lloyd and Norris 1999:
507), and also "medicalised explanations convey worthiness and, by association, funding" (516). Lloyd (2006) argues that "teachers and parents need
help in developing appropriately supportive interventions that take account

of what works for children with complex individual lives, not labels that lead to mass medication of children." (223). Lloyd also names the pharmaceutical companies as being active promoters of the medical model in order to expand their markets, and she accuses them of promoting "not only the widespread use of medication, but the professional mindset that views children in terms of normality and disorder" (220).

In their introduction to *Critical New Perspectives on* ADHD, Lloyd, Stead and Cohen expose the risks involved with prescribing drugs for young people, such as over-prescription and illegal use and sale of certain drugs. They indicate that medicating and prescribing are not carefully monitored for young children and there are no good studies completed on the effects of children taking stimulant medication long term. These scholars have discovered that there is evidence from the U.S. which indicates "an association with the continued use of psychoactive medication in adulthood" (2006: 2). Lloyd (2006) believes that attention to exercise may prove more beneficial than drugs in the long run, remarking that "the side effects of a good exercise program are far less invasive than the side effects of exposing children to long-term doses of medication" (224).

Cohen (2006) conducted a study in some Canadian schools to find out how and why the decision to medicate children is made. The study was conducted by a social worker researcher and three medical colleagues. The focus group consisted of parents, teachers, school-based psychosocial professionals and physicians who specialized in the assessment and care of children. Cohen was not impressed with the results, which indicate that parents felt pressured by schools to consult physicians, and physicians, for the most part, recommended medication. No one in the study was satisfied with the assessment process. There does seem to be some concern about the use of medication but little attempt to provide other types of intervention. Cohen reports: "The findings described a poorly controlled process of assessment, intervention, and follow-up lacking *explicit* guiding or consensus principles" (151, emphasis in original). He is also concerned that there have been so few long-term studies completed in the United States on the effects of treatment of ADHD. He says that an analysis of the few studies completed show that "from a scientific point of view, most positive effects attributed to ADHD treatments are exaggerated" (28). He adds that there is not much evidence that stimulants help children achieve academically and that stimulants affect all children who are given them (sometimes for performance enhancement), not just those diagnosed with ADHD. Cohen declares: "It is difficult, if not impossible, to find historical precedents for medically sanctioned mass drugging of youth to alter their behavior or improve their performance" (29).

Tait (2006) deplores the fact that we have been manipulated by society into believing that every character flaw, every weakness, every behaviour problem signifies a disorder and has a medical solution. Instead of working to find solutions for difficult behaviour problems, we take the easy way out and dispense a pill. Tait suggests that in schools, "the vast majority of behaviour disorders, including ADHD, appear to be treated pharmacologically. So, to put it another way, teaching life will be easier because disruptive students, quiet students, or generally different students, will be drugged into normalcy and passivity" (94). Tait concludes that is our way of getting everybody to fit into the norms that society has created. This may make the job of schools easier, but he wonders whether or not it is ethical, since it does away with moral responsibility.

Cooper (2001) is one of the scholars who believes that medication may be beneficial to children, but he feels that it should be used in conjunction with other interventions. One of its greatest benefits, he suggests, is that it is very effective in reducing core symptoms so that the child is able to benefit from educational programs. Castro (2003), a teenager who had been diagnosed ten years previously, testifies from personal experience that medication helps children to focus and, therefore, to achieve academically. But she admits that medication also has negative effects. It causes her to withdraw socially and to become uninterested in interacting with her friends, as well as dulling her imagination and creativity. She describes the personality change that occurs in her when she is on medication for ADHD:

> I am a totally different person on it than off it. This is called emotional lability. While on the medicine in school, I rarely ask my friends what there is to do on the weekend. At lunch I literally sit at a table without saying a word, and because of that I have lost a whole bunch of friends.... But when I am off my medicine I am this outgoing, spontaneous, hilarious person.... I am hysterically funny with my parents and a lot more imaginative in playing with my younger sister and brother. (2)

The negative side effects suppressing creativity, imagination and intellectual curiosity are also noted by Baum and Olenchak (2002), Cooper (2001), Kohn (1998), McMenamy, Perrin and Wiser (2005), McCluskey and McCluskey (2003) and Roberts (2004). As well as, the researchers argue that taking the medication because of having been labelled ADHD convinces children there is something wrong with them. They often feel stigmatized and blame themselves for the diagnosis. Kohn (1998) and Roberts (2004) believe that it is the teacher that profits the most from the medicating of children, because it turns the children into docile creatures. Kohn warns, as well, that it helps only in the short term, that it does not work for everybody and that we still do not know the long-term effects of taking medication for ADHD. This does not seem to deter those determined to view ADHD as a medical problem and to promote drugs as the best solution.

Diagnosing ADHD

Similar to the manner in which some scholars from different countries have questioned the validity of ADHD, so too in recent years, are some seriously taking issue with the way ADHD is diagnosed or misdiagnosed. They are finding that the whole issue of ADHD diagnosis seems to be a mass of contradictions (since several countries arrive at the diagnosis from very different perspectives), evasive and indefinite language (such as *may be, appear to be, seem to be* and, *thought to be*) and possibly false assumptions about children by experts who do not appear to know how to interpret their behaviour.

Yet, it is only too obvious that many professionals are convinced that ADHD has neuro-biological origins and that medication is a viable treatment. The United States, a country with a lot of influence throughout the world, views ADHD mainly from a medical perspective. Canada appears to be following the lead of the United States. Due to the ease with which information is disseminated through the Internet, many other countries are being persuaded toward the American point of view. The DSM-IV-TR, which, as previously stated, is the main diagnostic reference of the American health profession, describes ADHD as "a persistent pattern of attention and/or hyperactivity-impulsivity that is more frequently displayed and more severe than is typically observed in individuals at a comparable level of development." (2000: 85) Some of these features must have been present in the individual before the age of seven, and medication is the traditional treatment. But, as mentioned, this scientific reference has changed the criteria of ADHD during revisions, and uses inconclusive terms when describing the symptoms, such as *may, often* or *typically*, which causes some scholars to question the certainty of the medical diagnosis.

The National Institute of Mental Health (NIMH), which is part of the National Institute of Health, a section of the United States Department of Health, has released a booklet on ADHD, which recognizes it as a medical condition and follows the guidelines laid out in DSM-IV-TR for establishing a diagnosis. This booklet does admit that ADHD is not easy to diagnose "because the symptoms vary so much across settings" (2004: 2). Some symptoms, mentioned in this booklet, which lead to the diagnosis, include restlessness, fidgeting, having trouble waiting in line, blurting out, being easily distracted and difficulty following instructions. The NIMH points out: "Different symp-toms may appear in different settings depending on the demands the situation may pose for the child's self-control" (2). The booklet also mentions that these symptoms, displayed by children being assessed for ADHD, may disappear "if they are doing something they really enjoy" (3). The NIMH advises the family that suspects a problem with a child to seek help from an expert who has train-ing "in ADHD or in the diagnosis of mental disorders" (4). The NIMH states that specialists, in forming the diagnosis, must do a very thorough evaluation of the child in order to assess the severity of the symptoms, comparing the person's type of behaviour "against a set of criteria and characteristics of the disorder as listed in the DSM-IV-TR" (3–4). The NIMH assures parents that "there is little compelling evidence at this time that ADHD can arise purely from social factors or from child-rearing methods. Most substantiated causes appear to fall in the realm of neurobiology and genetics" (6). This publication goes on to report that extensive studies have shown that ADHD can be treated successfully with either a combination of behavioural management and medication, or medica-tion alone. The NIMH suggests also that many adults suffer from ADHD and that diagnosis can be difficult. There are assessment tools known as the Conners Rating Scale and the Brown Attention Deficit Disorder Scale, which can help with adult diagnosis, leading to treatment and relief from the problem.

In the United Kingdom, although the medical model is being promoted, many scholars lean more toward considering ADHD from a sociological per-spective. According to Davis (2006), some professionals in the field of child study "have suggested that children's behavior is rooted in social causes" (47), such as poverty, changes in family structure, changes in the education system, which demands higher standards and increased student performance, the in-troduction of national testing and student assessment, and changes in society caused by globalization. They argue that medical solutions of ADHD do not treat those root causes. Davis (2006) finds fault with both approaches toward diagnosis. He sees school restructuring to develop more inclusive practices as a possible solution but is also aware that, at the same time, demands for increased standards could cause more children to be diagnosed as ADHD (52). Davis speculates that the reason for increasing numbers of children being diagnosed may be tied in with the inability of the school to include children who don't fit with the "specific norms that are required to boost attainment" (53), along with the inability of the adults involved in assessing children to interpret their behaviours correctly. Davis contends that the children themselves should be actively involved with adults in articulating their difficulties and in finding a solution to their problems, instead of being passive bystanders. He is in favour of a more holistic approach toward diagnosis, one that involves "children, parents and carers at the child's school, ... assessment by educational/clinical psychologists and social workers, and takes into account cultural factors in the child's environment" (58).

Cohen (2006) is of the opinion that acceptance of ADHD as a valid childhood disorder has opened the floodgates, observing that the "diagnosis of ADHD and the drug Ritalin marked the beginning of the full scale psychiatric colonization of childhood. Today not only ADHD, but the whole range of psychiatric labels... are now applied to children, some of whom are barely old enough to talk" (29).

Jacobsen (2006) does not believe that the display of ADHD behaviours on the part of children signifies a disorder. Instead he suggests it may indicate a power struggle between children and adults, and he asks: "Is the diagnosis of children as ADHD yet one more tool adults are using to try to enhance their power over children?" (171).

However, other researchers have a different view of the diagnosing process. Baum and Olenchak (2002); Cooper (2001); Cramond (1994); McCluskey and McCluskey (2003); and Montague, Mckinney, Hocutt and Harris (1992) are convinced that early diagnosis is critical for effective intervention. These authors suggest that the purpose of the diagnosis is to bring an awareness to educators of the child's unique learning style so that a program can be developed geared to individual needs. Specht (2002) points out that the diagnosis is necessary in order to access funding which will make individual programs possible, which suggests that the label may be used for political purposes. She adds that the emphasis should be on more research into ways that children achieve and, like Lloyd, would prefer less emphasis on diagnosis and labelling (6). Cramond (1994) and McCluskey and McCluskey (2003) believe that the label will have positive consequences if the child's individual strengths and talents are recognized as a result of the diagnosis.

Tied in closely with diagnosis is the danger of misdiagnosis, which Walker (2006) maintains is the situation with American "Indian" children who have been diagnosed with ADHD. Walker insists that the diagnosis is invalid because assessment is based on Euro-American values rather than on those of Indigenous culture. Walker observes that the assessment does not take into consideration their different learning style, which uses a hands-on approach. He contends that behavioural symptoms are caused by cultural conflict. In the case of these children, says Walker, experts are "diagnosing intergenerational trauma, grief and oppression as ADHD" (70). This wrong diagnosis leads to "the continued segregation of 'Indian' children, lowering expectations regarding their academic potential, deepening a self-concept of inferiority, and encouraging parents and caregivers to put them on stimulant drugs" (70).

A further problem with misdiagnosis, according to Baum and Olenchak (2002), is that it often leads to more tests and more labels for the child as well as disagreement among professionals as to the best type of intervention, resulting in possible damage to the child.[1] Sometimes children with other exceptionalities, they add (gifted, for example) exhibit behaviours similar to those of ADHD and, when wrongly diagnosed, may suffer because of being placed in a remedial program rather than a challenging one.

Kohn (1998) is highly critical of the whole diagnostic process involving ADHD, seeing it as badly flawed, because there is no consistency in the way the three behaviours judged to be present in ADHD (inattentiveness, impulsivity and hyperactivity) are assessed. Assessment can be very subjective, since everyone has different level of tolerance for those particular behaviours.

Marshall, a Foucauldian scholar, is convinced that the classifying of individuals as certain kinds of learners is manipulative, dominating and enslaving (cited in Peters and Burbules 2004: 67). He disagrees with any type of diagnosis that results in labelling. The majority of the scholars who have completed recent research are not at all happy with the manner and the frequency in which ADHD is diagnosed, likening it almost to the wrongful conviction of children, a judgment with which Walker would, doubtless, wholeheartedly agree.

Inclusions and Exclusions

Foucault, in his books and lectures, has alerted us to the many ways that our society, while ostensibly advocating *inclusion*, actually promotes and practices *exclusion*. As previously stated, he deplores the manner in which human beings have been made into objects by society through the use of dividing practices (such as labelling), which give them "both a social and personal identity" (cited in Rabinow 1984: 8). Foucault indicates that this mode of objectification is widespread in many public institutions, but especially prevalent in schools, and he defines "dividing practices" as "modes of manipulation that combine the mediation of a science (or pseudo science) and the practice of exclusion — usually in a spatial sense, but always in a social one" (8). When he alludes to "pseudo science," he is referring to the human sciences, which, according to Peters and Burbules (2004), he alleges are one of the "modes through which human beings have been constituted in Western culture as both subjects and objects of knowledge" (41). According to Foucault's definition, attention deficit hyperactivity disorder (ADHD) qualifies as a "dividing practice," since the label is generally the result of a series of tests and observations conducted by pediatricians, psychologists and other professionals in the education field, usually sets the children apart from their classmates and causes them to be treated as the *other* in the education system. Foucault charges that institutions which classify, stigmatize and exclude people in this way are practising "political violence" (cited in Rabinow 1984: 6).

Lipsky and Gartner (1997), who have written extensively on the need for inclusion and school reform, agree with Foucault's conclusion, suggesting that the school's practice of categorizing children and, thereby, excluding them, does more harm to children than the condition for which they are categorized. According to the literature on the subject of inclusion, there is increasing recognition by those in society who have children's well being at heart that any type of segregation in the classroom is detrimental to the growth and development of children and is unacceptable (Lupart 1998; Porter 2004; Slee 2001). There is an extensive body of literature which outlines the meaning of inclusion (Thousand and Villa 1995; Porter 2004; Slee 2001; Dixon 2005), details the problems involved in implementing inclusion (Hutchinson 2007; Lloyd 2006; Howes Booth, Dyson and Frankham 2005), elaborates on parents' attitudes toward inclusion (Leyser and Kirk 2004) and enumerates ways of developing inclusive classrooms (Lupart 1998; Porter 2004, Lloyd 2006; Hutchinson 2007). Most of the research is directed toward the inclusion of all children, rather than those who manifest a specific condition such as ADHD, and it establishes a general consensus on the need for inclusion in today's classrooms. However, there seems to be some disagreement among education experts as to the how the concept should be interpreted and incorporated throughout the education system.

Villa and Thousand give their interpretation of inclusive education:

> The word *include* implies being part of something, being embraced into the whole. *Exclude*, the antonym of *include*, means to keep out, to bar, or to expel. … The very meaning of the terms *inclusion* and *exclusion* helps us to understand inclusive education. … Inclusive education is about embracing all, making a commitment to do whatever it takes to provide each student in the community… an inalienable right to belong, not to be excluded. (1995: 6–8)

Thousand and Villa further define inclusion in the classroom as "the practice of welcoming, valuing, and supporting the diverse needs of all students in shared general education environments" (1999: 73). Dixon states it even more succinctly:

> Inclusive classrooms are that which the name implies — classrooms where all students are included regardless of abilities or disabilities. This inclusion is not just a physical inclusion, that is, students sharing

the same physical space, but also a mindset.... Inclusion is first and foremost a state of mind. (2005: 35)

Smith, Polloway, Patton and Dowdy (1998) maintain that the classroom teacher is the most important element in ensuring that the child is *of* not just *in* the class. This opinion is shared by Schwean, Parkinson, Francis and Lee (1993) and Sciutto, Nolfi and Bluhm (2004), who feel that the attitude of the teacher is crucial. Not only does the teacher have a great deal of influence on the child, but the teacher can also influence the attitude of the whole class. Schwean et al. observe that, "although teachers are in a position to be an ADHD student's ally, they also have the power to seriously debilitate a student" (2003: 43).

Howes, Booth, Dyson and Frankham (2005), in their research paper "Teacher Learning and the Development of Inclusive Practices and Policies," also concentrate on teachers and the problems they encounter in implementing inclusive practices. These researchers suggest ways to overcome such problems, suggesting that "inclusive practices are those which tend to reduce barriers to learning and participation for *all* pupils" (2005: 146, emphasis in original) and that "the process of a school becoming more inclusive involves teacher learning" (133). They note that some of the obstacles to inclusive practice that teachers face are "the narrowing of the curriculum, the focus on targets and groups on the borderline of meeting those targets, the categorization of pupils in terms of a narrow conceptualization of attainment and the de-democratisation of schools" (137). However, teachers can be challenged to examine their practice in light of inclusive values, which is not easy for them to implement because teaching is such a demanding profession. One of the ways this may be possible is through the process of social learning, which can be a valuable tool. This can be accomplished through visits by researchers and staff from other schools, who observe pupils, interact with them and interpret their findings in joint staff groups. This process can be enlightening for teachers as "taken-for-granted assumptions can be and are recognized and questioned, prejudices subject to reflection, and the value of structures questioned and addressed" (135). Howes et al. argue that outsiders such as researchers and visiting teachers can be a valuable resource to a school in promoting inclusion.

For Porter, inclusive schooling means that "children go to their community or neighbourhood schools and receive instruction in a regular class setting with non-disabled peers who are the same age" (2004: 2). He maintains: "Our children need to be educated in heterogeneous classrooms where the diversity of students is welcomed, celebrated and nurtured" (2). He believes that "by educating our children together, in socially inclusive groups, we help ensure consistently better outcomes" (3). He argues that "schools need to reject the approach best described as 'traditional special education,'... an approach that continues to segregate and isolate children who are different" (3). Although Canadian schools have made great strides toward inclusion, it is still available only for some children and in some circumstances; for Porter, that is not good enough. As a means to ensure that all children receive a quality education, he proposes that class sizes be kept reasonable and teachers receive adequate support in terms of training, planning time and provision of para-professional supports. Porter asserts that we need to adopt "a clear vision for inclusion that represents the 21st century reality of Canada, and the 21st century aspirations of Canadians" (4), but we will need the structures and funding mechanisms in place to make that vision a reality.

Hutchinson agrees wholeheartedly with Porter's recognition of the necessity for Canada to be a model for inclusion, explaining that "participating in all facets of society, including educational institutions, is a fundamental right of all Canadians" (2007: 4), and "educators in all other countries look to Canada's commitment to inclusion as a model and inspiration" (xix). But she also recognizes that successful inclusion in classrooms presents a challenge and has caused controversy among teachers, who have conflicting views on inclusion and assumptions about children who do not fit the norm. Some teachers welcome only students who can keep up with the curriculum and see problems with modifying the curriculum for those who are unable to do so. Other teachers see benefits from inclusion for every student in the class. Hutchinson argues that research shows that the attitude of the principal is of utmost importance. The research reveals that "teachers who are effective in inclusive classrooms tend to have principals who believe that all children can and should learn in regular classrooms and that teachers should adapt their modes of instruction rather than expect exceptional children to adapt" (19). In Foucault's terms, the intersection of knowledge and power means that when leaders support inclusion, teachers will be more likely to adopt and support inclusive practices. Hutchinson understands, as well, the daunting task facing teachers who implement inclusive education. They must identify the needs of the learner, keep records, collaborate with school-based teams, help develop individual education plans and liaise with parents. In order to provide the greatest benefits for all children, she advises beginning teachers to ask themselves: "How do I adapt my teaching to include these exceptional individuals?" and not "How do I individualize for these students?" (xx).

Lupart is concerned that, although Canadian schools are making progress in supporting inclusive education, there are still barriers and inequalities. She argues that "before authentic progress toward inclusion can be realized, three key areas of education need to be reviewed and transformed" (1998:

2). These key areas concern policy, organization and legislation. She argues as well, that "there must be a shift from charity-like compensation and exclusion to acknowledgement of human rights and inclusion" and that "for inclusive education to work, all educators must be prepared to assume responsibility for all students in the school community" (4). Lupart says that some teachers are unwilling to do that without necessary classroom support. She feels that regular classroom teachers' concerns have not been heeded and that "if inclusive education becomes a reality in schools, it will be because regular classroom teachers have accepted full responsibility for student diversity and are willing to make classroom adjustments necessary to promote learning by all students" (6). Lupart submits that there will have to be school reorganization, the roles of the regular teacher and the special education teacher will have to be merged, and teachers will have to learn to work together to solve problems. As well, says Lupart, the government has to fulfill its role by providing necessary funding for classroom support and for research. Lupart suggests that "universities and academics in faculties of education, specifically, may be in a key position to effect needed change" since those institutions train teachers, engage in and publish research, and are removed from and independent of school boards and government departments (10). They can be instrumental in helping education systems solve their problem of how to achieve "equity and excellence" (4).

Lloyd considers the issue of inclusion in schools in Britain: "The research also clearly indicates that some schools exclude more children than others, even when they have very similar student populations. The ethos, curriculum, discipline and support systems of schools are highly significant in understanding why some schools are able to be much more inclusive" (2006: 216). She adds that during the seventies and eighties there was a move to see disability as a social construction and to treat students "as whole human beings." This led toward educational inclusion. But she sees now, in Britain as well as the United States and many other parts of the world, a strong move to classify ADHD as a medical condition with pharmaceuticals as the main treatment. This puts the focus on the child and not on the school environment. The move toward inclusive schools now is "accompanied by the medicalisation of children's behaviour and by ever larger demands on special education budgets" (220) but, Lloyd suggests, it is also accompanied by teacher anxiety because some feel they don't have the skills to help these so-called "special needs" students. The reason for their anxiety is that there is a great deal of literature which reminds teachers that students with ADHD "are distinctly different and that teachers will need particular advice as to how to manage them in the classroom." The "pedagogical approach" must be "tailored to the disability or disorder" (221).

Lloyd states that this view has now been challenged through explorations of different pedagogical approaches, by Lewis and Norwich (2000), who conclude that there is a move away from the idea that children with "special needs" need a special kind of teaching and a move toward the idea that "what works for most pupils works for all pupils though there might be differences in application" (cited in Lloyd 2006: 221). Lloyd argues that what is needed are just caring and supportive teachers who can construct "appropriate and meaningful learning experiences" for all children, who can "develop pedagogy that is inclusive of all students' (222–3). Lloyd suggests that teachers have to be flexible, able to provide a varied curriculum, well organized and skilled in classroom management. She firmly states that there is no requirement of special technology; rather, "involving students in cognitively based activities where they identify their own solutions and construct their own programs encourages engagement with educational processes" (224–5).

Leyser and Kirk (2004) take a different approach in their research. They conducted a study on the attitude of parents of children with a disability toward inclusion, and it revealed that the majority of parents support inclusion although they have grave concerns about teachers' instructional skills in inclusive education. Leyser and Kirk agree that this concern is valid since teachers themselves feel they have not enough training. Leyser and Kirk indicate that parents are also concerned about their child's social acceptance in the classroom but observe that there are social skills training programs offered, and there is a need for ongoing programs of that sort. They suggest that parents' views and ideas should be an essential component of an ongoing evaluation of any inclusion program.

Slee, in his discussion of several papers which deal with inclusion (which he views as a "grand and elusive" concept), presents "four sets of dilemmas" (2001: 113) relating to inclusion. First, there are the different meanings people attach to the concept of inclusion. He feels that "we need to say what we mean at the outset and to challenge the meanings attached to inclusion by others" (116). Slee clearly defines what he means by inclusive education: "Inclusive education is not about special educational needs, it is about all students" (116). Second, there is the tendency in discourse to define the person according to a disability, which tends to negate the rest of the person. Slee suggests: "In reducing the person to the textbook accounts of defectiveness we deny possibilities for learning and active citizenship lying within their complexity" (117). Third, in inclusive educational research, the voices of those most affected are silenced, since most research is determined by non-disabled people, thus presenting an incomplete picture of disability. Fourth is the difficulty of preparing teachers to practise inclusive schooling. Slee concludes by reminding us that "we need to continue to be reflective about both the theory and practice, which are indivisible of inclusive schooling"(121).

The literature details the barriers which prevent our education system from fully embracing the concept of inclusion as envisioned by Villa and Thousand (1995). It shows that while authorities have adopted this ideal notion of inclusion in theory, in practice, they have not adequately supported it with the necessary funding and supports. The literature demonstrates as well that those in society who have children's well being at heart increasingly recognize that any type of segregation in the classroom is detrimental to their growth and development and is unacceptable (Lloyd 2006; Porter 2004; Lupart 1998). As long as schools give lip service to the concept of inclusion by placing children of all abilities in the same physical space but excluding some from a full range of participation, thus furthering the distance between those considered "normal" and those who are not, children will suffer. This approach is exclusion in the guise of inclusion, making it a mockery by turning it into a "dividing practice." It is a form of "political violence," against which Foucault urges us to protest. Everyone involved needs to understand the violence visited on the child by such exclusionary practices, along with other actions which may lead to the isolation of children, such as I.Q. testing and all manner of labelling, including ADHD.

McCluskey and McCluskey (2003) and McLeskey and Waldron (2000) offer a broad view of what inclusion should mean for those who are seen as "different" in the classroom. They maintain that if children diagnosed as ADHD are viewed as individuals with unique strengths and talents and if these strengths and talents are welcomed in a classroom which embraces diversity and sees difference as a gift rather than a disorder, then the children will flourish and use these differences as an opportunity for growth and fulfillment. And surely providing our children with opportunities to experience growth and fulfillment should be the ultimate goal of our education system. Any education practice that violates that goal by denying children all the benefits of inclusion falls under Foucault's definition of "political violence" and should be met with public protest. Baum and Olenchak (2002) sum up the dichotomy pertaining to inclusion that is prevalent in our education system by asking a pertinent question: "Is education's purpose to unearth and nurture each student's strengths, or is it to find weaknesses, and regardless of the toll on the individual, pander to them?" (89–90). If the answer to the first part is in the affirmative, then we are on the road to Villa and Thousand's (1995) model of inclusion. However, if our goal is to find weaknesses, then we are on a treacherous path of testing, labelling, dividing and other exclusionary practices, a path that often leads to discrimination and marginalization. Is what we want for our children?

Since there are so many conflicting opinions over the origins and treatment of ADHD, and even over its validity as a physical condition, it clearly is a very complex issue. Whether seeing ADHD as a medical disorder, a social construct, a method of exerting power over children or simply a different learning style, all scholars agree that the school has a significant role to play in shaping the child's social and personal identity. They stress that acceptance and a sense of belonging are necessary in order to establish a healthy self-image. As Cohen (2006) asserts, discrimination, marginalization and exclusion have no place in "the only institution designed exclusively for children."

Note

1. This was Ben's experience.

Chapter Six

IT IS BETTER TO LIGHT A CANDLE

And from my neck so free
The albatross fell off, and sank
Like lead into the sea.
(Coleridge, 1798, *The Rime of the Ancient Mariner*)

I believe too much in truth not to suppose that there are different truths and different ways of speaking the truth. (Foucault, quoted in Tamboukou and Bal 2003: 14)

Like the Ancient Mariner, I have told my story to those "who cannot choose but hear." I have presented my version of the truth of ADHD. I would like to think that I am freed from my albatross, that the readers of this book (especially educators), like the wedding guest, are now "sadder and wiser," that they will accept my interpretation and make the necessary changes in education practices. However, in the words of Foucault, "I believe too much in truth not to suppose that there are different truths and different ways of speaking the truth." And I have discovered, as I reflect back on my life, that the pursuit of truth is neither simple nor straightforward. Nothing is exactly the way it seems. So much depends on perspective. There are many ways of looking at issues such as labelling, learning, education and freedom of choice in a disciplinary society. Truth is multifaceted. I have looked at it and for it through different lenses, as a grandmother telling Ben's story, as an educator comparing practices of different eras, as a feminist reflecting on the status of mothers in society and, over all, as a post-structuralist applying a Foucauldian lens to the problem of "truth" in today's world, as I consider how "regimes of truth" are established. Somehow during this process, my investigation into the truth of ADHD seems to have metamorphosed into an indictment of the education system because of its practice of subjugating children, as well as an indictment of society as a whole for its continued subjugation of women while professing their liberation.

When I was a young mother during the sixties I came across an interview in a magazine article with the wife of the president of the United States. She was trying to stay out of the political limelight and concentrate on raising her young children. What she said resonated deep within me and stayed with me over all these years because it was exactly the way I felt then about the responsibility of parents for their children and remains the way I feel now about the responsibility of society for all children. The gist of her words was this: *If we fail our children, if we do not do our best by them, it does not matter how well we succeed in any other area of life.* This is a truth which has greatly influenced me throughout the years. And it is the reason I tell my story; I am convinced that society by way of the school system is failing many of our children. Governments continue to under-fund education. Big business seems to run our world. Values are decidedly questionable.

Learning should be a joy for all children. The realization that our schools often induce the very opposite effects, through not treating children equally, by excluding and marginalizing them, was brought home to me in a powerful way through my grandson's experience. I have always, in some dim recess of my mind, been aware of inequalities in our patriarchal society, of the way some groups are privileged over others, but I never really delved deeply into how such situations came about, assuming that this is just the way things are. You don't mess around with the status quo.

Foucault changed my thinking drastically. He helped me to see that things have not always been this way and that you should mess around with the way things are if it affronts your sense of justice or fairness, because the status quo is just one of the regimes of truth created by society. And it can and needs to be changed. Until recently I was hesitant to rock the boat, content to sit in my "comfortable pew" and let someone else debate the issues. An introverted person such as myself needs a serious issue which affects her personally, a sense of the moral rightness of her stand and a lot of support as incentive to speak out. Ben's traumatic experience in the school system was the catalyst that turned me into a "Raging Granny." And it was Foucault's theory concerning the fluidity of truth, and the way in which it is always embedded in power relations — the relationship between power, right and truth "which is organized in a highly specific fashion" in our society (1980: 93) — which gave me the impetus I needed to critique the ADHD phenomenon. As I witnessed Ben's growing unhappiness and the gradual erosion of his self-esteem, I became very angry, mostly at his teachers for not recognizing his intelligence, for treating Ben with disrespect, for taking away his dignity — so angry that I managed to overcome the inhibitions of a lifetime and go public with his story in order to expose the many truths of ADHD. By telling Ben's story, by providing a glimpse into Ben's life, I hope that the voices of other children will resonate and be heard as well. It is now my aim to make people aware that something has gone awry in the education system, and not in the children who travel through the system, and that things can and must be changed.

My research led somewhat to the evaporation of my anger at the teachers, since I quickly learned that, in spite of the way it looks from the perspective of parents of children like Ben, the teachers are not the villains in the school system. Because they are the front-line workers, in most cases they are the scapegoats. They are as much victims of the system as Ben was, as are all the Bens in the school who have suffered similarly. They have too large classes, too few supports and too little control over what they teach and how they teach it. They must go along with the policies of the administration even if they have serious misgivings. Speaking as an educator, Gail Jardine (2005) reminds us:

> It often can feel like we do not have the power to teach what we think it is vitally important for them to learn, nor can we teach them in the ways that would, in our professional judgment, be the most beneficial to them now and in the future. (3)

Jardine's statement appears to be slightly at odds with the prevailing belief that we have significantly improved our school practices and thus the education of our children during the past thirty or more years. We have heard a great deal about educational reform, but as Popkewitz (1991) suggests, "*reform* is a word whose meaning changes. ... Nor does reform signify progress, in any absolute sense" (emphasis in original: 2). He adds that we must be "skeptical of what we or others call progressive" (244–5). Many people look back with nostalgia but also with a considerable degree of scorn at the era of the one-room school, administered by members of the community, where one teacher with few teaching aids was responsible for many different grades, but that system allowed the teacher a great deal of freedom. There were no experts to advise the teacher. Children walked to school and romped freely with each other on the playground. That was the era during which I received my education. It would appear that we have really progressed, now that we have big regional schools, one-grade classrooms, buses to transport the children, all manner of technological devices to expedite learning and a proliferation of education experts who classify our children as certain kinds of learners. But have we progressed? As a person who both learned and facilitated learning in a one-room school, I, like Popkewitz, am slightly skeptical. I have no desire to turn back the clock. Like Foucault, I must refuse "to sentimentalize the past in any way or to shirk the necessity of facing the future as dangerous but open" (cited in Rabinow 1984: 27). However, we have lost a great deal of educational freedom in the name of progress. Our schools are now caught in the web of our disciplinary society. They are locked into a system that is rigidly run and tightly controlled by cumbersome school boards far removed from their communities and staffed with individuals skilled in the art of doublespeak. Instead of offering teachers more in-classroom support, some school boards hire more psychologists who continue to assess and label children, perpetuating many of the issues raised in this book. Communities also seem to have lost control of their children's learning. Teachers, as well, have lost control over what they teach, yet they are held accountable for children's learning. Children are manipulated by educational psychologists into classifications and categories which can determine as early as the junior high level their future acceptance into university. Their freedom to choose is limited. Is this progress? The era during which my children went through the school system probably comprised the best of both worlds. Government had just begun to pour money into education, and school boards were new and had not started to flex their muscles. There were modern buildings and buses for transportation, but schools and teachers still had a certain degree of autonomy. The psychologists had not yet begun to pathologize children's behaviour. Children like Larry escaped Ben's ordeal. They were simply considered intelligent, active children and were free to become what *they* felt capable of becoming. We must take a hard look at certain more recent school practices such as testing and classifying children as "learning disabled," "developmentally delayed," ADHD or any other label. We must question whether or not our children's learning experience has been enhanced by these practices.

Not only does my personal story reveal the way new practices in education, viewed as signs of progress, can impact negatively on children, but it also unmasks the way new regimes of truth in society have a negative impact on women, particularly in their role as mothers. Women of my generation were told "a woman's place is in the home." We knew exactly where we stood in light of society's expectations. Today's message to women is much more ambiguous. On the one hand, our culture tells women they are emancipated, free to embrace any profession, free to combine a professional career with that of homemaker and parent, free to be the consummate professional, wife and mother all in one, or free to concentrate on the role of stay-at-home parent. On the other hand, conditions in society, such as costly and insufficient daycare, lack of understanding by employers and inequalities in salaries, have made life incredibly challenging for working mothers, yet inadequate compensation for stay-at-home parents, along with a lack of respect for those who choose full-time mothering over a career, has made that choice difficult as well. Society, in ostensibly giving women more choices, has led women to be more critical of their own performance. In this way, they are falling victim to Foucault's third mode of objectification, which Rabinow calls "subjectification" (1984: 11). They spend their lives trying to mould themselves into society's vision of the perfect mother, the perfect wife and the perfect career woman. Many exhaust themselves trying to be superwoman because society tells them that since they are free to "have it all," they must excel in all areas. I think it is in the role of mother that women, since the eighties, find themselves caught most securely in the web of power and knowledge which our disciplinary society has woven around the concept of mothering almost from the moment of the child's conception. The hold psychology has on our culture along with the tremendous advances in technology are mainly responsible for this situation. Through modern technological devices, babies are tracked and assessed in the womb. Before and after birth, there is a standard of weight, height and development against which they are measured. Pity the poor mother whose baby falls into the lower percentile! This was my daughter-in-law's experience. That combination of knowledge and power caused her at times to feel like an unfit mother even before her child was born. And that feeling of being measured and found wanting is often experienced by women who are mothering in this era, because now, as Foucault contends:

> We are in the society of the teacher-judge, the doctor-judge, the educator-judge, the "social-worker" judge; it is on them that the universal reign of the normative is based; and each individual, wherever he may find himself, subjects to it his body, his gestures, his behaviour, his aptitudes, his achievements. (cited in Jardine 2005: 53)

The manner in which psychology has been allowed to dictate the standards considered normal, concerning the growth, development and learning capabilities of children, as well as the prevailing attitude by society that mothers are somehow to blame if children fall below those standards, makes life very difficult for mothers of children like Ben. They know that their children are intelligent and capable, but their knowledge is disqualified in favour of the scientific evidence of tests and observations by so-called experts. When they continue to fight for their children's educational rights they are branded throughout the school system as troublemakers or worse. No wonder they sometimes willingly accept the label ADHD for their children; it provides an escape from the blame and shame heaped on them for parenting a child who does not conform. It is indeed a label of forgiveness. Our culture extracts a heavy price from women for the "freedom" they supposedly possess.

Reflecting on my life story has shown me that there are no easy answers to questions of truth and freedom in today's world. But Jardine articulates Foucault's belief that we need to converse with others, to try to understand and respect other points of view while reserving the right "to remain unconvinced, to perceive a contradiction, to require more information, to emphasize different postulates, to point out faulty reasoning" (Foucault, cited in Jardine 2005: 120). By engaging in such conversations with others, we

> risk and challenge what each of us holds as truth.... Taking this risk

and facing this challenge will allow each of us to tell the truth about ourselves and listen to the truth of others in ways that have the potential to transform our modern western systems of knowledge and power. (122)

As Foucault has demonstrated, every human being is objectified to some extent and subjected to the combined forces of power and knowledge in our society. And his suggestion as to a way out of this dilemma is "to refuse what we are. We have to imagine and to build up what we could be.... We have to promote new forms of subjectivity through refusal of this kind of individuality" (quoted in Rabinow 1984: 22). Jardine clarifies Foucault's statement further: "He urged us all to identify and fight the forces that turn us away from our own rich life experiences and instead bring about our own objectification" (2005: 8).

Marcus reminds us that this is not an easy process: "It requires the capacity for courageous, honest self-critique, 'thinking differently,' risk-taking and other practices of freedom. It also requires ... facing tough emotions" (2008: 130). Ben has done this. It took some time, but he has finally shed the negative self-image and the feelings of worthlessness which his years in the school system imposed on him. In his mid-twenties he now sees himself as an intelligent, capable person. He has at last stepped out from under the shadow of ADHD and is regaining his trust in learning institutions. This was a lengthy process, and one that I had hoped would happen over time. I hope now that those who hear Ben's story will be "more critical of the presumed rationality of our discourses and practices" (Baynes et al. 1987: 97). I realize that as one person challenging the ideas surrounding ADHD, I may not be able to bring about much change, but, as Burke (1729), the eighteenth-century statesman and philosopher suggests, "It is better to light a candle than to curse the darkness."

EPILOGUE

I started writing, read it over, erased it, started again and erased it all. Finally, I gave up and sort of just let it evolve. I think that there is so much that could be written about the impact of ADHD on my life that it is difficult to condense it into a few paragraphs and give a true picture of how I felt at the time.

Looking back on my schooling experience I can say that there were some good times and some bad. Being labelled ADHD was not the worst of the problems I had in school. In fact to me it wasn't really a problem at that time. To me it was a good excuse as to why I wasn't succeeding in all the areas the other kids were. When it came to math I remember just not getting it and being scared to ask the teacher for help after she had already explained it to me twice. Being ADHD was a relief in a way, because I could blame ADHD for the reason I wasn't getting things and not really blame me. But as a young kid going through his years in school I couldn't understand what that would do to me, or the role it would later play in the way I handled things in my life.

In hindsight I can see the downward spiral throughout my school years. It started by me being excited to go to school every day, excited to learn new things, even excited to have homework. By the time I was in grade twelve I hated school and barely ever went. The time between grade two and grade twelve was filled with constant struggle. I rejected school, and in turn most teachers (not all) rejected me. I didn't get a high school diploma. It turned out that I was short one class but never bothered taking that class. I was ready to move on and never think about school again.

I worked random jobs for a few years after high school, one of them being in a treatment centre for adolescent kids. I put four years into that place and enjoyed being able to help other people out. I also travelled Europe, lived and worked with family in Ireland. It was while travelling that I thought about going back to school again. All the history in Europe interested me, so I went to Mount Royal University in Calgary and signed up as a mature student. After a year and a half there as an unclassified student, I transferred into a B.A degree at the University of Lethbridge.

In September 2011, I started my fourth year of a B.A. in history. After I finish that I'm not sure where exactly I'll end up. I've thought about law school or going into teaching. If I were to pursue a career in teaching, it would be at the university level. Right now I am just focusing on what is in front of me.

Ben Stordy

REFERENCES

American Psychiatric Association. 2000. *Diagnostic and Statistical Manual of Mental Disorders: DSM-IV TR*. Washington, DC: Author.

Armstrong, T. 2006. "Canaries in the Coal Mine: The Symptoms of Children Labeled 'ADHD' as Biocultural Feedback." In G. Lloyd, J. Stead and D. Cohen (eds.), *Critical New Perspectives on ADHD*. London & New York: Routledge.

Baker, B.M. 2001. *In Perpetual Motion: Theories of Power, Educational History, and the Child*. New York: Peter Lang.

Ball, S.J. (ed.). 1990. *Foucault and Education: Disciplines and Knowledge*. London and New York: Routledge.

Barkley, R. 2002. "International Consensus Statement on ADHD." *Clinical Child and Family Psychology Review* 5(2): 89–111.

Barthes, R., and L. Duisit. 1975. "Introduction to the Structural Analysis of the Narrative." *New Literary History* 6(2): 237–72.

Baum, S., and R. Olenchak. 2002. "The Alphabet Children: GT, ADHD, and More." *Exceptionality* 10(2): 77–91.

Baynes, K., J. Bohman, and T. McCarthy (eds.). 1987. *After Philosophy: End or Transformation*. Cambridge, MA: Cambridge University Press.

Bigge, M.L., and S.S. Shermis. 1999. "How Does Bruner's Cognitive Interactionist, Narrative-Centered Cultural Psychology Treat Learning and Teaching?" In *Learning Theories for Teachers*, sixth edition. Toronto: Longman.

Britzman, D.B. 2000. "The Question of Belief: Writing Poststructural Ethnography." In E.A. St. Pierre and W. Pillow (eds.), *Feminist Poststructural Theory and Methods in Education*. New York and London: Routledge.

Bruner, J. 1990. *Acts of Meaning*. Cambridge, MA: Harvard University Press.

Castro, J. 2003. "I Am a Different Person." *Time,* November: 58.

Clandinin, D.J., and F.M. Connelly. 2000. *Narrative Inquiry: Experience and Story in Qualitative Research*. New York: Jossey Bass.

Cohen, D. 2006. "Critiques of the 'ADHD' Enterprise." In G. Lloyd, J. Stead, and D. Cohen (eds.), *Critical New Perspectives on ADHD*. London & New York: Routledge.

Coleridge, S.T. 1970 [1798]. *The Rime of the Ancient Mariner*. New York: Dover Publications.

Conrad, P. 1975. "The Discovery of Hyperkinesis: Notes on the Medicalization of Deviant Behavior." *Social Problems* 18(1): 12–21.

_____. 1992. "Medicalization and Social Control." *Annual Review of Sociology* 18: 209–32.

Conrad, P., and W.S. Schneider. 1980. *Deviance and Medicalization: From Badness to Sickness*. St Louis & Toronto: C.V. Mosby.

Cooper, P. 2001. "Understanding AD/HD: A Brief Critical Review of Literature." *Children and Society* 16: 387–95.

Cramond, B. 1994. "Attention-Deficit Disorders and Creativity: What Is the Connection?" *Journal of Creative Behaviour* 28(3): 193–209.

Davis, J. 2006. "Disability, Childhood Studies and the Construction of Medical Discourses: Questioning Attention Deficit Hyperactivity Disorder: A Theoretical Perspective." In G. Lloyd, J. Stead, and D. Cohen (eds.), *Critical New Perspectives on ADHD.* London & New York: Routledge.

Dixon, S. 2005. "Inclusion-Not Segregation or Integration Is Where a Student with Special Needs Belongs." *Journal of Educational Thought* 39(1): 33–54.

Dumm, T.L. 1996. *Michel Foucault and the Politics of Freedom.* Thousands Oaks, CA: Sage Publications.

Ellis, C., and A.P. Bochner. 2000. "Autoethnography, Personal Narrative, Reflexivity: Researcher as Subject." In N.K. Denzin and Y.. Lincoln (eds.), *Handbook of Qualitative Research,* second edition. (Thousand Oaks, London, NewDelhi: Sage Publications.

Foucault, M. 1979. *Discipline and Punish: The Birth of the Prison.* New York: Vintage Books.

____. 1980. *Power/Knowledge: Selected Interviews and Other Writings 1972–1977.* (C. Gordon, ed.). New York: Pantheon Books.

____. 1982. "Truth, Power, Self: An Interview with Michel Foucault." In L.H. Martin (ed.), *Technologies of the Self: A Seminar with Michel Foucault.* London: Tavistock.

____. 1987. "Questions of Method: An Interview with Michel Foucault." In K. Baynes, J. Bohman, T. McCarthy (eds.), *After Philosophy: End or Transformation.* Cambridge, MA: Cambridge University Press.

____. 1990 [1978]. *The History of Sexuality: An Introduction* (Vol. 1). (R. Hurley, trans.). New York: Vintage Books.

____. 1997 [1994]. *Ethics: Subjectivity and Truth.* (P. Rabinow, ed.). (R. Hurley & others, trans.). New York: New Press.

Funk, C.E. (ed.). 1955. *Funk & Wagnall's New Practical Standard Dictionary of the English Language* (Vol. 1.) New York: J.G. Ferguson Publishing.

Grantham, M. 1999. Etiology of Attention Disorders: A Neurological/Genetic Perspective. (Electronic version retrieved March 2005). Educational Resources Information Center. ED 436 912.

Harwood, V. 2006. *Diagnosing Disorderly Children: A Critique of Behaviour Disorder Discourses.* London and New York: Routledge.

Howes, A., T. Booth, A. Dyson, and J. Frankham. 2005. "Teacher Learning and the Development of Inclusive Practices and Policies: Framing and Context. *Research Papers in Education* 20(2): 133–48.

Hutchinson, N.L. 2007. *Inclusion of Exceptional Learners In Canadian Schools: A Practical Handbook for Teachers* (second edition.). Toronto: Pearson Prentice Hall.

Jacobsen, K. 2006. "ADHD from a Cross-Cultural Perspective: Insights into Adult-Child Power Relationships." In G. Lloyd, J. Stead, and D. Cohen (eds.), *Critical New Perspectives on ADHD.* London and New York: Routledge.

Jardine, G.M. 2005. *Foucault and Education.* New York: Peter Lang.

Kirk, S.A., and H. Kutchins. 1992. *The Selling of DSM: The Rhetoric of Science in Psychiatry.*

New York: Aldine De Gruyter.

Kohn, A. 1998. "Suffer the Restless Children: Unsettling Questions about the ADHD Label." In A. Kohn *What to Look for in a Classroom... and Other Essays*. San Francisco: Jossey-Bass.

Larner, W., and W. Walters. 2004. *Global Governmentality*. London: Routledge.

Leyser, Y., and R. Kirk. 2004. "Evaluating Inclusion: An Examination of Parent Views and Factors Influencing Their Perspectives." *International Journal of Disability, Development and Education* 51(3): 271–85.

Lipsky, D.K., and A. Gartner. 1997. *Inclusion and School Reform: Transforming America's Classroom*. Baltimore, MD: Paul H. Brookes.

Lloyd, G. 2006. "Supporting Children in School." In G. Lloyd, J. Stead and D. Cohen (eds.), *Critical New Perspectives on ADHD*. London & New York: Routledge.

Lloyd, G., and C. Norris. 1999. "Including ADHD?" *Disability and Society* 14(4): 505–17.

Lloyd, G., J. Stead, J., and D. Cohen (eds.). 2006. *Critical New Perspectives on ADHD*. London and New York: Routledge.

Lupart, J. 1998. "Setting Right the Delusion of Inclusion: Implications for Canadian Schools." *Canadian Journal of Education* 23(3): 251–66.

Maclure M. 2003. *The Fabrication of Research: Discourse in Educational and Social Research*. Philadelphia, PA: Open University Press.

Marcus, P. 2008. "Valerie Harwood, Diagnosing 'Disorderly' Children: A Critique of Behaviour Disorders Discourses." (Review). *Foucault Studies* 5: 128–30.

McCluskey K.W., and A. McCluskey. 2003. "ADHD: Disorder or Gift? "*Journal of the Gifted and Talented* 16(1): 32–42.

McLeskey, J., and N.L. Waldron. 2000. *Inclusive Schools in Action: Making Differences Ordinary*. Virginia: Association for Supervision and Curriculum Development.

McMenamy, J.M., E.C. Perrin, and M. Wiser. 2005. "Age-Related Differences in how Children with ADHD Understand Their Condition: Biological or Psychological Causality?" *Journal of Applied Developmental Psychology* 26(2): 111–31.

Miller, P., and N. Rose. 2008. *Governing the Present*. Cambridge, UK: Polity Press.

Montague, M., J. Mckinney, A. Hocutt, and J. Harris. 1992. "Attention Deficit Disorder and Learning Disabilities." *Exceptionality Education Canada* 2(3/4): 75–90.

Nadesan, M.J. 2010. *Governing Childhood into the 21st Century: Biopolitical Technologies of Childhood Management and Education*. New York: Palgrave MacMillan.

National Institute of Mental Health. 2004. "Attention Deficit Hyperactivity Disorder." Online. Retrieved March 17, 2008 from <http://www.nimh.nih.gov/publicat/adhd.cfm>.

Norris, C., and G. Lloyd. 2000. "Parents, Professionals and ADHD: What the Papers Say." *European Journal of Special Needs Education* 15(2): 123–37.

Ongel, U. 2006. "'ADHD' and Parenting Styles." In G. Lloyd, J. Stead and D. Cohen (eds.), *Critical New Perspectives in ADHD*. London & New York: Routledge.

Peters, M.A., A.C. Besley, M. Olssen, S. Maurer, and S. Weber. 2009. *Governmentality Studies in Education*. Rotterdam, The Netherlands: Sense Publishers.

Peters, M.A., and N.C. Burbules. 2004. *Poststructuralism and Educational Research*. Lanham, Boulder, New York, Toronto, & Oxford: Rowman & Littlefield.

Polkinghorne, D.E. 1988. *Narrative Knowing and the Human Sciences.* New York: State University of N.Y. Press.

Popkewitz, T.S. 1991. *A Political Sociology of Educational Reform: Power/Knowledge in Teaching, Teacher Education, and Research.* New York and London: Teacher's College, Columbia University.

Popkewitz, T.S., and L. Fendler (eds.). 1999. *Critical Theories in Education: Changing Terrains of Knowledge and Politics.* New York & London: Routledge.

Porter, G. 2004. "Meeting the Challenge: Inclusion and Diversity in Canadian Schools". *Education Canada* 44(1). (Retrieved online March 2008.)

Rabinow, P. (ed.). 1984. "Introduction." *The Foucault Reader.* New York: Pantheon Books.

Rafalovich, A. 2001. "The Conceptual History of Attention Deficit Hyperactivity Disorder: Idiocy, Imbecility, Encephalitis and the Child Deviant, 1877–1929." *Deviant Behaviour* 22(2): 93–115.

Roberts, W. 2004. "Ritalin in Schools: A Tool to Compensate for Insufficient Educational Resources?" *Crosscurrents* 8(1): 20–23.

Rose, N. 1998. *Inventing Ourselves: Psychology, Power, and Personhood.* Cambridge, UK: Cambridge University Press.

Schrag, P., and D. Divoky. 1975. *The Myth of the Hyperactive Child: And Other Means of Child Control.* Pantheon Books.

Schwean, V.L., M. Parkinson, G. Francis, and F. Lee. 1993. "Educating the ADHD Child: Debunking the Myths." *Canadian Journal of School Psychology* 18(1-2): 55–90.

Sciutto, M.J., C.J. Nolfi, and C. Bluhm. 2004. "Effects of Child Gender and Symptom Type on Referrals for ADHD by Elementary School Teachers." *Journal of Emotional and Behavioural Disorders* 12(4): 247–42.

Slee, R. 2001. "'Inclusion in Practice': Does Practice Make Perfect?" *Educational Review* 53(2): 113–23.

Smith, T.E.C., E.A. Polloway, J.R. Patton, and C.A. Dowdy. 1998. *Teaching Students with Special Needs in Inclusive Settings.* Second edition. Boston: Allyn and Bacon.

Specht, J. 2002. "Educating Exceptional Children: Current Issue for Educators." *Education Canada* 44(1): 2–8.

Tait, G. 2006. "A Brief Philosophical Examination of ADHD." In G. Lloyd, J. Stead, and D. Cohen (eds.), *Critical New Perspectives on ADHD.* London & New York: Routledge.

Tamboukou, M., and S.J. Ball. 2003. "Genealogy and Ethnography: Fruitful Encounters or Dangerous Liaisons?" In M. Tamboukou and S.J. Ball (eds.), *Dangerous Encounters: Genealogy & Ethnography.* New York and Washington: Peter Lang Publishing.

Tennyson, A. 1854. "The Charge of the Light Brigade." In C. Ricks (ed.), *The Poems of Tennyson.* London: Longmans, Green.

____. 1898. *The Poetic and Dramatic Works of Alfred Lord Tennyson.* Boston & New York: Houghton Mifflin.

Thousand, J., and R.A. Villa. 1999. "Inclusion: Welcoming, Valuing, and Supporting the Diverse Learning Needs of all Students in Shared General Education Environments." In S. Pfeiffer and L. Reddy (eds.), *Inclusion Practices with Special*

Needs Students: Theory, Research, and Application. New York: Haworth Press.

Villa, R.A., and J.S. Thousand. 1995. *Creating an Inclusive School.* Alexandria, VA: Association for Supervision and Curriculum Development.

Walker, D. 2006. "ADHD as the New 'Feeblemindedness' of American Indian Children." In G. Lloyd, J. Stead and D. Cohen (eds.), *Critical New Perspectives on ADHD.* London & New York: Routledge.

Walshaw, M. 2007. *Working with Foucault in Education.* Rotterdam, The Netherlands: Sense Publishers.

Woodrum, D.T. 1994. "ADHD Training Modules for Rural Health Care Providers, Educators and Parents." (Electronic version retrieved March 2005). Educational Resources Information Center. ED 369 362.